THE DUELLISTS

PEP, JOSE AND THE BIRTH OF
FOOTBALL'S GREATEST RIVALRY

First published in English by deCoubertin Books Ltd in 2017.

First Edition

deCoubertin Books, Studio I, Baltic Creative Campus, Liverpool, L1 OAH
www.decoubertin.co.uk

ISBN: 978-1-909245-48-8

© 2016 Baldini&Castoldi - Milano

English translation Copyright © De Coubertin Books Ltd, 2017

A CIP catalogue record for this book is available from the British Library.

Cover design & typeset by Thomas Regan at Milkyone Creative.

Translation by Anthony Wright.

Printed and bound by Opolgraf.

THE DUELLISTS

PEP, JOSE AND THE BIRTH OF FOOTBALL'S GREATEST RIVALRY

PAOLO CONDO

Translated from the Italian by Anthony Wright

CONTENTS

INTRODUCTION

LUIS FERNÁNDEZ HAS NEVER BEEN THE SORT OF person to pick a fight with.

When he was nine years old, his mother loaded him and his five siblings into their clapped-out car and took the family from Tarifa, a town on the southernmost tip of Spain, from where it is possible to see Tangier across the Strait of Gibraltar, to Lyon in search of fortune. They grew up in a classic *banlieue*. He went to school in one of the districts populated by the first waves of migrants, and football became like an escape route for him. Luis had endless energy and was physically powerful, although on one occasion after he had been called an *espingouin* – a derogatory name for Spanish emigrants – once too often, he beat up the person that had called him it and earned himself a six month exclusion.

However, it was this sort of upbringing that made him into the linchpin of that great France side of Michel Platini, Jean

Tigana and Alain Giresse. If anyone went in too hard on one of his more technically gifted team-mates, Luis was the first to arrive on the scene, his face menacing, and ready to do anything to defend them.

People like that don't lose their edge when they become a manager. I remember one night in the spring of 1996 when Paris Saint-Germain were celebrating their Cup Winners' Cup victory in a beautiful hotel in Brussels. The club's owner had called upon the legendary Yannick Noah to motivate the team, and, under the disdainful eye of Luis, the former tennis player (and rock star, restaurateur, playboy and all-round guru of French sport) spoke to the team on several occasions in the days leading up to the game against Rapid Vienna. That night a group of journalists, a group which I was able to sneak into, smiled at Fernández's entirely unsympathetic impressions of Yannick, who was busy in the next room entertaining the Parisian VIPs and charming their wives and girlfriends. Many journalists give Noah a lot of the credit for the cup victory, which remains the club's only European trophy even after so many years backed by the sheikhs. Luis – who had smelt a rat for some time – chose the height of the celebrations to announce he was leaving for Athletic Bilbao, and received a warm send-off. The backdrop to this story occurs at San Mamés a few months later, when Bobby Robson's Barcelona arrived to face Fernández's side for a difficult La Liga match.

It was a stellar Barça side, although they were only able to enjoy the talents of Ronaldo for that single season, as the following summer Massimo Moratti made him the biggest signing of his Inter presidency at that point. Alongside *O Fenomeno* was the unstoppable Luís Figo, the wily Gheorghe Popescu, the killer Fernando Couto, the centre back Miguel Ángel Nadal (who would occasionally bring his nephew Rafael to games, even though he was already a Real Madrid supporter), the tireless Luis Enrique, the precise Iván De La Peña and, of course, their captain Pep Guardiola. On the bench alongside the experienced Bobby Robson was a stylish, good-looking young man who had a perpetually sullen demeanour. Officially, his role was the English coach's translator, but he had actually already been promoted to the first team's coaching staff. He seemed to be full of youthful exuberance, flicking frantically through the notes piled next to the head coach, who, in comparison, sometimes looked a bit lethargic. Over time we've learned that José Mourinho's body language is an integral, indivisible part of his personality: he doesn't use it to convey a message, but it is instead part of the message itself. At the time, of course, this was all completely unknown to Luis Fernández, who grew increasingly angry from his position on the bench at La Catedral, where the first commandment is 'don't let anyone bully you in your own house', as he watched the young Portuguese celebrate wildly following Abelardo's opener. When José Mari made it 1-1 midway through the second half Luis sprang into life, urging the Basque fans – who aren't the quietest anyway – to roar the Leones on even more vociferously, and when Julen Guerrero fired a superb free kick into the far corner 15 minutes from the end, inevitably he ran to celebrate in front of the opposition bench. There was nothing much in that. But what the future Special One couldn't stomach was his lecturing, the finger pointing, and the insults. Mourinho got up from his position on the bench, his finger menacingly jabbing at Fernández's face, and his provocation certainly got to Luis – who up until then had been very heated but not violent – as it then took a couple of people to restrain him.

Generally words drift away on the breeze in stadiums, but in some they can fester, particularly those that have narrow players' tunnels, which can become a powder keg waiting to explode. It certainly did on this occasion; at full time Mourinho found himself surrounded by Basques – among whom was a certain Aitor Karanka, who we will meet again soon – and only Figo was there to stand up for him. Elsewhere, simultaneously, Guardiola suddenly appeared alongside Fernández.

'Don't laugh at other people's defeats,' the Barcelona captain shouted in the Athletic coach's face, and while the physical contact between the two was brief it was intense. Had it been anyone else, Luis would have raised his hands to shove them away, or more likely punch them. But Pep Guardiola was not just anyone else, and the Barcelona captain's personality was such that the temperamental coach remained civil in his reply. As he spoke to him, he made it clear that it was the Portuguese who had prompted all the anger. He quickly justified himself: in his own stadium, with the adrenalin of victory pumping through his veins, and in a situation where others had already started scuffles, Luis Fernández explained the reasons for his anger to the hieratic Guardiola, who even then was something of a warrior monk. Their encounter lasted just a few seconds: as he was being spoken to, Pep looked ahead of him, staring daggers at the Athletic players surrounding Mourinho and Figo, but he then forced the two Portuguese ahead of him as they walked towards the dressing room to avoid any further confrontations, like naughty children slinking away from a fight to avoid further punishment. His intervention was successful and was achieved with pure charisma: he didn't raise a hand, he didn't make any threats, just using the weight of his own leadership.

●

IN THE 1977 FILM THE DUELLISTS, RIDLEY SCOTT'S masterful directorial debut, the meeting between Armand d'Hubert (Keith Carradine) and Gabriel Feraud (Harvey Keitel) came about because the former, sent by a leader of the Napoleonic army, needed to place the latter under house arrest for taking part in an illegal duel. However, Feraud took offence at how he was given the news and d'Hubert was eventually challenged to a duel, accused of cowardice if he didn't accept. As the story progresses, it's quite clear that d'Hubert is on the side of reason and Feraud on the side of (depraved) wrongdoing, but it's not this that forms the parallel between the story of the two officers and the rivalry between Pep Guardiola and José Mourinho. It's the clash of personalities. D'Hubert is cold, magnanimous, superior and detached like Guardiola. Feraud is proud, stubborn, hot-tempered and over the top like Mourinho. When they face each other, their vices and virtues are driven to extremes as they each assume their role in the story. Pep is considered to be a figure of perfect sportsmanship, the flawless and fearless knight who offers his hand to his opponent before and after the battle. Mou, meanwhile, subscribes to the football equivalent of Italian minister Rino Formica's definition of politics as 'blood and shit'; that is what the fans hunger for, and it's no coincidence he's loved by them.

It's possible that the help Guardiola gave him in Bilbao, opportune yet also seen in some obscure way as humiliating, is the starting point of their rivalry. Mourinho denies this suggestion, but given that he also denies that their patently obvious rivalry exists at all, you can't give that too much credence. Conversely, it's nearly impossible to talk about Mou with Guardiola. He was left broken by his mental battle with the Portuguese during the two seasons they faced each other in Spain, which even forced him to take that famous sabbatical in New York – a break from the game that was unprecedented in the career of a top coach. Anything to avoid hearing people talk about Mourinho. However, there was a moment of sincerity in an answer he gave to a question on the eve of the Clásico in 2012, when I surprised him by asking him whether in 20 years' time (citing Alexandre Dumas) he would go out for dinner with Mourinho and talk about their past duels. Both Pep and José are given coaching before major press conferences: one of their colleagues bombards them with the most uncomfortable, nasty questions that might come up so that they are in a position to give an adequate response. My question, which was neither uncomfortable nor nasty, just humane, visibly put the Catalan coach on the back foot. At first he mumbled, 'Right now it would be unthinkable, of course, but in 20 years' time...' and then, touched by a moment of inspiration, he said more certainly, 'Yes, I would like to, I think we'd both like some answers to a lot of things that we're curious about.' Most of which occurred in those turbulent 18 days between 16 April and 3 May, 2011.

ONE

YOU ALWAYS FEEL STRONG EMOTIONS WHEN you see him again. Especially when he's in a foul mood, because then it's like a typical case of Stockholm syndrome: you can't help but feel both attraction and fear at the same time. You've got to love José Mourinho. He's a Grand Theft Auto character who's been transported into the real world. He's so over the top that he's a caricature of himself, but there's nothing like being there to listen to him insult and mock Spanish journalists as he tells you how lucky you are. If you want to go to a Lady Gaga gig, you have to pay. If you want to go and see the latest show on Broadway, you have to pay. If you want to eat at San Lorenzo, sat on the next table to Victoria Beckham, you have to pay. But it's free to watch Mourinho's performances, and with a journalist's pass you can even see him live. And when he wants to put on a show, he never fails to perform.

On the eve of the first of the series of four Clásicos, the journalists who report on Real Madrid were given the news that assistant manager Aitor Karanka – yes, that Karanka – would be holding what promised to be a dull press conference, and they controversially left the room without asking any questions. Mourinho couldn't let this sort of insubordination happen again: seeking retribution is one of his core principles. He made himself available for the post-game press conference for the same game, giving Alvaro Larrosa of *AS* an opportunity to ask him what he had thought of the referee's performance that night . He glowered at him, giving him an effortless look of disdain. 'Are you the editor of *AS*?' No José, he's certainly not the editor, he's a lamb that they've sent to the slaughter. You have to be patient when Mourinho is tearing into you – if you survive the experience, then maybe you'll become a real journalist. 'I'll ask you again: are you the editor?' Once the unfortunate guy – imagine being in his situation – confessed, dejectedly, that he wasn't the editor of the second biggest sports paper in Madrid, José dismissed him with a well-rehearsed speech. 'I don't have to answer you. If you won't talk to my assistant then according to your philosophy I can only talk to the man in charge as well.' As if the whole scene was following a pre-prepared script, the next person to speak, a journalist from *Punto Pelota*, was one of the few who hadn't left the press conference at Valdebebas the day before. He also asked Mourinho about the referee, as if nothing had happened, and while his colleagues looked at him contemptibly, Mourinho completed his check-mate. 'I'll answer you, even if you aren't the editor, because I respect you, just like you showed respect yesterday to a professional who deserved it, a man called Aitor Karanka, who is fully employed by Real Madrid.' Then, in response to a journalist from *Marca* who was deluded in thinking that he would now be given the benefit of the doubt, he said just one word: 'Inda.' Send me Eduardo Inda, your editor.

Mourinho is the only top coach who allows his coaching staff to speak frequently to the media, and the regularity of Karanka's appearances in the Valdebebas press room wasn't a surprise to those of us who were used to seeing the genial Beppe Baresi holding court at Internazionale's training ground at Appiano Gentile instead of the cutting Portuguese. José has often said that, if he could, he would only speak to the press once a month at most, but given the way he carries himself, that is unlikely to be true: eight of the first 10 things that one might remember about him will have been said in front of a microphone. Just like his body language, the way he constructs what he says isn't a way of expressing his message, but is the message itself. To keep everyone highly strung, which is a crucial aspect of his management style, every press conference has to contain a strong message which people will talk about for days, which will unite those on his side and will wind up the opposition. And seeing as how it isn't humanly possible to come up with such a controversial message in every press conference, when Mourinho doesn't feel like he has one up his sleeve then he delegates the task of talking about the squad's mindset on the eve of a game to his assistant, aware that no one will say anything significant and thereby disappointing the gathered journalists, for whom the mere fact of covering Mourinho normally gives their paper a good headline. It's the quickest way to make a career for themselves: José knows this, and expects them to be amenable to his outbursts in return. When there's a note of discord in the air – which happens a lot in Madrid, where even the humblest of reporters feel like they are austere descendants of the grand traditions of Real Madrid – then Karanka appears in the press room. On their first day together, he and Mou very probably brought up the subject of that night in San Mames, when the no-nonsense Aitor cornered José and was ready to smack him. His new boss certainly gave the Basque his forgiveness, but only in exchange for absolute obedience and unwavering loyalty. Stories from deep within the Madrid dressing room recount that, in those days, Karanka used to pace up and down repeating, 'We're the much stronger side, Barcelona are a media invention.' There's no problem with the first part, any motivator would approve of that, but the second part is cause for concern as not even the most blinkered observer could convincingly argue that sort of nonsense.

But what brought Mourinho to the point where he entered into an argument about editors? It was the evening of 16 April, 2011, and the first of four Clásicos to be played in 18 days had just finished 1-1 at the Bernabéu. Barcelona were essentially La Liga champions, as they sat eight points clear with six games to go, but it was the first time since Pep Guardiola had taken over as the Blaugrana coach that he hadn't beaten Real Madrid. After five consecutive wins – among which were the humiliating 2-6 win at the Bernabéu in his first season and the *manita*, the 5-0 victory earlier in the season – the draw was a small signal that the tide might be turning. It was a fair result, because while on the one hand Mou had gift-wrapped the match by starting the intimidating Pepe instead of the creative Ozil in midfield, on the other hand Barça had created very little, thereby justifying this tactical change. As they passed the ball around, Real set themselves up with two lines of defence, each made up of five players, with Ángel Di María even filling in at full back. The Argentine, who had been signed earlier that season from Benfica, was making his El *Clásico* debut, and as we'll soon see he made sure his presence would be felt.

Like Messi, Di María was born in Rosario, and is so slight that he has been nicknamed 'Fideo' (the noodle). He follows a tradition of thin players started by *César* Luis Menotti: 'el Flaco' was proof in South America that physique was no boundary to ability. Di María was the knight on Mourinho's chessboard: an unpredictable and dangerous piece, gifted with a different way of moving to everyone else that made him (almost) unstoppable. That night, for example, midway through the first half of a game that was drifting aimlessly, it was he who tried to take the initiative when he received a crossfield ball played more in hope than expectation by Sami Khedira. The two teams were retreating back to the midfield after an unsuccessful Madrid corner when the German intercepted the ball and played it out to the left hand side. The intention was to give his side more time to get back, but Di María transformed it into an opportunity thanks to his two pincer-like legs. As the ball flew out towards the far touchline he brought it down smartly before taking it under control and accelerating towards goal. As Ángel got into the penalty area, chased by a crowd of opponents, he should have gone towards the byline to then try and pull the ball back towards the penalty spot to pick out one of the world class finishers in the team.

Instead, he was too tempted by the idea of going it alone and his curling left-food shot ended up in the crowd. It came to nothing, but symbolically the chance, which had come out of nothing, showed that there was a difference about this Madrid, impetuous and fully recovered from the previous malaise that they had suffered from ever since Guardiola had taken charge. This time, faced with the Catalans' hypnotic passing once again, Real appeared to have the answers. Marcelo ran down the left hand side with his head always up, looking around to see what was ahead of him and trying to pick out a pass for Ronaldo. This is a crucial aspect of football: players' movements are not always particularly synchronised – when it's not perfect, a gap will suddenly open up before closing again just as quickly. If you don't see that gap straight away, then a moment later you wouldn't even know it had been there. At one point Marcelo played a sensational pass to Ronaldo, and his fiercely hit ball was so unexpected and so inspired that Cristiano, amazingly, miscontrolled it, allowing Adriano to step in and clear the ball away from danger. A small detail. But was it not Mourinho himself who defined the Champions League as 'the tournament of details', meaning that there is often very little between the top sides? There was another example of this, from the same player, in the last minute of the first half: Sergio Ramos leaped high above the Catalan defence to meet a deep corner, and the ball looped towards the far post for Ronaldo to get a good header on it. It was probably too good. As Cristiano got into the perfect position to meet it, it gave Adriano the precious fractions of a second he needed to get back onto his own goal line and head the ball clear. Half time came and, while the score suggested Barça were still in control, it also suggested

Real Madrid had shaken off their inferiority complex.

This new self-belief was soon required in the second half; after Raúl Albiol was sent off for fouling Villa, Messi converted from the penalty spot to put Barcelona in front. In the past this would have been fatal, but this Real side were stronger psychologically. Their attitude while playing with 10 men against 11 led them to within a whisker of a goal when Seydou Keita's intervention caused Pepe to miss the target before they were awarded a penalty themselves, as clear as the first, when Dani Alves brought down Marcelo late on. Ronaldo placed it into the corner, a much more convincing finish than Lionel Messi's – whose penalty Iker Casillas had nearly reached – and even this had a small mental impact on the contest. Real Madrid's first draw after so many defeats was, psychologically, a victory, if you also take into account that they came from behind with 10 men, and it allowed Mourinho to leave the Bernabéu in a good mood. This game was the least important of the four, considering that the league was as good as over, and consequently it was psychologically at the heart of the Portuguese's strategy: he needed to stop a seemingly endless run of defeats before the momentum could really be turned in the opposite direction.

As a result, when the final whistle sounded, both groups of players had something positive to take from the game: Real had stopped the rot and Barça were closer to winning the title. But the run of four Clásicos, which was made possible once the Champions League draw had been made more than a month before and had been confirmed when they had brushed aside the opposition in their path (Tottenham Hotspur and Shakhtar Donetsk respectively), had caused tensions between Madrid and

Barcelona to boil over, with the result that even the players' relationships were breaking down almost irreparably, despite the fact that many of them were international team-mates.

To get off the pitch at the Bernabéu, both teams have to descend down a few steps before climbing up the stairs towards the dressing rooms: the stairway is also divided by a metal grill, which adds a gladiatorial tone to the atmosphere. Just before the stairs there is a small open area, and it's there where the excitement and the emotions of the game can spill over. When you're delighted at getting the draw because you feel like the moral victors, nothing enrages you more than finding out your rivals feel the same way. Winning and losing are defined by their very nature, and the points gained clearly indicate who can enjoy the result and who is demoralised by it. The draw, however, is a grey area – especially, almost uniquely, in football, where its complexities are increased – as anyone can convince themselves that they have the upper hand. But when you think you've won on points, seeing the same, smug expressions on the opposition's faces is like a gust of wind destroying a house of cards.

There are many different versions of what happened in the couple of minutes after the final whistle. Some say that the brawl started when Gerard Piqué, an ardent supporter of Catalan independence, shouted in his opponents' faces: 'Spagnoletti [little Spaniards], on Wednesday we're going to Valencia to take the cup away from your king.' Others say that Pepe tried to punch Messi, sparking a furious melee. Still others say that Rui Faria, Mourinho's other assistant, was like a man possessed, insulting Barça's players for their theatrics on the pitch and enraging them so much in that stairway that they tried to take matters into their own hands. Whatever may have happened, the 18 days of war – the preparation for which, as we've seen, will have started a long time before – were inaugurated by a bar room brawl. Guardiola tried to calm things down in the Catalans' dressing room. Some players' knuckles were bleeding after trying to throw punches through the grate, Puyol was breathing heavily after trying to separate his Spanish team-mates from coming to blows with each other, some – as they had already done during the game – were lamenting the fact that the grass on the Bernabéu pitch was long and dry, claiming it was unsportsmanlike from Real. It was certainly not unintentional: Mourinho had been telling the groundsmen all week not to cut the grass and to water it as little as possible, keeping the sprinklers tightly sealed, particularly on the day of the game. The idea had come following that 5-0 defeat in November that had left Mourinho mentally wounded: the first goal, which immediately set the pattern for the game, came from yet another moment of brilliance from Andrés Iniesta, who sliced open an almost perfectly arranged defence with a miraculously precise pass to pick out Xavi. What did he need to find the only possible route through four Blancos defenders? Essentially, three things: a surgeon's dexterity, and Iniesta could operate with his feet; a pass that was weighted more like a shot, and in fact Xavi did extremely well to control the ball before beating Casillas; and a surface on which the ball could run perfectly, and the Camp Nou has a surface like a billiard table. Of these three things, Mourinho only had the ability to influence the last, and intervene he did. He definitely intervened. On the night of 16 April, the grass at the Bernabéu was more than 100mm long, while the average length – which is used for the national team's matches – is 25mm. Four times less. Barça's players were furious because their passing game relied on having a pitch where the ball could run easily, and after explaining this to their coaching staff they told everyone who had a microphone in the mixed zone, triggering the war on grass: the next day it was impossible not to notice the shocked tones of the Catalan newspapers and the mocking tones of the Madrid press. There were even cartoons devoted to it, with Pepe drawn chasing Messi through grass that was taller than both of them, like two kids running through fields of wheat.

TWO

IN PREPARATION FOR THE COPA DEL REY FINAL on Wednesday 20 April, Barcelona's directors asked for, and were quickly granted, the same pitch preparation as for national team games. The grass at the Mestalla – Valencia's ground, where the game was to be played – would be cut on Sunday afternoon, twice on Monday, twice on Tuesday, twice on Wednesday before the game, and once more half an hour before kick-off. If it didn't rain (as the forecast suggested it would) it would then be watered for nine minutes. The fact that there was so much controversy about what was undoubtedly just a technicality – shorter grass favoured Guardiola's style, so it was entirely in Mourinho's interest to keep it as long as possible – was a clear indication that the situation was rapidly escalating towards all out war. There were two factors that delineated the sides' respective positions: the power struggle, where Barcelona were generally perceived to hold the upper hand, and the two coaches' different psyches. Mourinho attacks, provokes, causes controversy, partly because it's in his nature but mainly because he needed to break the unbeatable aura of calm around Barcelona and their coach. The more the contest seemed like a fencing duel, the less chance Real had of beating the odds; however, if Mourinho was able to get under Guardiola's skin, turning it into a mud fight, his chances increased exponentially. Pep wins on a level playing field, to beat him Mou needs to create an intense atmosphere.

He worries Guardiola because he creates a maddening, almost unmanageable resistance to his idealistic world building. The way his Barcelona side played, which reached its apogee of style and efficiency in his third season, theoretically made no allowances for an opponent: it was harmonious, innovative, orchestral, scintillating, enthralling, even erotic in its foreplay – the possession that became known as *tiki-taka* – that climaxed with goals of dazzling, orgasmic beauty. There had never been anything like it, with the exception of Rinus Michels' Ajax and Arrigo Sacchi's Milan, the fathers of total football; but the Blaugrana orchestra was on another level, a booming wall of noise to their predecessors' strummed guitars. Guardiola maintained with some amount of false modesty that his mentor, Johan Cruyff, had painted the Sistine Chapel while his successors, himself included, were simply given the privilege of touching up small parts of the masterpiece as they began to peel away. Naturally that isn't true, because his numerous small restorations – such as the fusion of possession and pressing – will be studied on coaching courses for decades. But people have been convinced by Pep's modesty, because, as it is based on unquestionable results, it has since become the focus of the most banal comparison made whenever another coach says something brazen. 'How can you say that when you've won nothing, while Guardiola, who has won everything, keeps a much lower profile?' Pep is like a safety car for other coaches' egos, and the philosophical ideal that numerous other clubs around the world, including in Italy (Ciro Ferrara at Juventus or Clarence Seedorf, Filippo Inzaghi and Cristian Brocchi at Milan, for example), have tried to replicate by promoting a former player to become their coach. Who could resist introducing such a tempting system?

It must be resisted though. The magnificence of Barcelona's play, made perfect by having created it itself (there were games when all 11 players on the pitch had come through the club's famous youth academy, the *cantera*), was such a threat that the cyclical nature of football nearly ground to a halt when confronted by the dominance of their style. In this respect, Guardiola is right to see Cruyff's return to Catalonia as a coach, back in the late 1980s, as the birth of the project, and the intuition of using Leo Messi as a 'false nine' is a mix between the tactic's roots in the past and the opportunity to implement it again using the world's best player. It's ridiculous to think that this move can be replicated anywhere, but that hasn't stopped dozens and dozens of coaches from trying. Domination – at least culturally, which on its own is its introductory form – is just a step away .

●

SEEN FROM UP CLOSE, A CHANCE WHICH I HAD over breakfast (on the promise that I wouldn't quote him), Pep Guardiola has the charm of an unarmed prophet. He can't help but proselytise those who listen to his way of understanding football, sport, politics, or life; because he holds strong beliefs, he always has to assert himself. His humility, which he mostly proclaimed early on, is clearly a mental counterweight to his success. Or, perhaps more accurately, it's a safety valve which is triggered as soon as he breaks new records, which often happens – just think of the six consecutive trophies he won in his first 18 months. Talking to Guardiola is a challenge, because the speed of his reasoning is phenomenal, but it's a most fulfilling sensation during those times when you are able to stay with his train of thought: I understand, therefore I am worthy.

Mourinho is a profoundly different conversationalist but no less discerning, because his is a game of disguise: there could be different meanings behind every word, and it is only when they are all put together that their meaning suddenly become apparent, like finding the treasure at the end of a treasure hunt. This gift of cunning is no less seductive than the gift of intelligence. The difference is entirely within the philosophical aims behind them: Mourinho wants to win, while Guardiola wants to create. There's no doubt that the Portuguese coach's successes stem from his expert ability to put a team together, while the Catalan coach has created teams like no one else. But these are causes and effects, not the business itself. That's altogether different, because while Mou is convinced that the history books will be most concerned with lists of honours, Pep imagines himself at the centre of the conclusive final chapter, the one about the team that plays so well that theirs is deemed to be the definitive style.

●

THERE WERE TWO MORE CONTROVERSIES RAGING

in the build up to the Copa del Rey final, curiously caused by two world class Argentines who both, in their own eras, found their affirmations in Spain (more precisely, in one case, in Catalonia, which is very different): Alfredo Di Stéfano and Leo Messi. Marked by Pepe that Saturday with asphyxiating aggression, Leo proved he was human by letting a small sign of irritation show when, to take out his frustration after losing possession, he kicked the ball against an advertising hoarding on the edge of the pitch. However, his contact was less pure than usual: the ball clipped off the top of the advertising hoarding, flying into the first few rows of spectators. It was certainly clumsy, but Messi's intention was for the ball to bounce back onto the pitch. Real fans jumped to their feet to protest, but Leo had already turned around without paying attention to the insults, which were no different to anything else the Bernabéu crowd shouted at him. Maybe he realised something had happened when Pepe – patron saint of the offended – grabbed him from behind and made the *segno del matto*, putting his finger up to his temple as if to say there was something wrong in his head. He certainly realised when Sergio Ramos verbally insulted him, because while Ramos is temperamental, he isn't unfair. The referee Muñiz Fernández just about restored calm without booking Messi (seven yellow cards and a red were already enough, for the first game of the series), a decision which Mourinho only appeared to skim over in the press conference afterwards. While giving his answer to one of the few questions that were allowed, he laughed at Albiol's dismissal – which was correct; the foul on Villa in the penalty box was a clear goalscoring opportunity – but he had filed the incident away in his mind. 'We got on alright playing with 10 against 11, because we prepared all week for this scenario: I knew it would happen, it always happens to me against Barcelona, and I know it happens to Valencia too. I admit, once – just once – I would like the opposite to happen.'

The reference to the lack of a second yellow card for Messi was in the detail, and the next day the Madrid press butchered the referee for being influenced by the Argentine superstar's reputation. But that wasn't all the capital's newspapers had to say. *Marca*, the biggest-selling sports daily and notably partisan towards Real, contained a scathing article on Real's attitude towards the game by Alfredo Di Stefano. At 85 years old, Don Alfredo – the club's honorary president and close advisor to Florentino Pérez – was a kind of faded club figurehead. A few years previously, in 2006, I was in the main stand in the Bernabéu and witnessed a heart-wrenching scene. The great Ferenc Puskas, who had died that week, was remembered before a game against Racing Santander, and, as the moving music of Ennio Morricone sounded around the immense and emotionally-charged stadium, tears filled the eyes of the fans as their gazes focused on the other two members of that magical trio of the late 50s: Gento and Di Stéfano. Francisco Gento, the old Madridista winger, rose laboriously from his seat. Don Alfredo tried to bend his knees but to no avail; he remained seated with his flat cap raised in his left hand, his right gripping the hand of Gento. The ceremony lasted 90 seconds, 90 intense seconds, and, watching those two old men holding hands and saying goodbye to their friend of many years and many triumphs, there was the strong feeling of the passing of time, cruel and even offensive as it brought about the physical decline of old heroes.

Di Stéfano died in 2014 after dedicating his last years to his life's mission: the greatness of Real Madrid, of its traditions and of its values. Unsurprisingly, Mourinho's very defensive tactical outlook in the home league match upset him, and he told the *Marca* journalist who wrote down Don Alfredo's thoughts each week all about his disappointment, speaking about a lion (Barça) and a mouse (Real Madrid), about how the defensive attitude turned out to be the wrong one, about how the Catalans' superiority was plain for the entire world to see, and about a frustrating lack of personality from Real. These were serious accusations, given that not only were they being made by the club's greatest icon, but that they were also far worse than the words of Barcelona's standard-bearer Johan Cruyff, who had an easy task of writing in *El Periódico de Catalunya* (a newspaper aligned far more closly to Barcelona) that 'if Real welcome us by playing seven defenders at home, the compliment they're paying us is implicit' or that 'Mourinho is a negative coach, he only thinks about the result – he doesn't care about the game at all'. Serious criticisms, but they were to be expected and were taken into account. It was the friendly fire that caused more damage.

Naturally José was too intelligent to respond to Di Stéfano in his typically aggressive manner, or to just pretend that he hadn't read the article, which would imply a lack of respect to the greatest moral authority of the values of Real Madrid. 'Di Stéfano is everything to this club, and I am nothing,' he said, choosing his words carefully in the Mestalla press room before the Copa del Rey final. The press room can be like trying to trap a bolt of lightning: this time it was Guardiola who went first in the running order – fundamental to planning attacks or ripostes – and, as per his normal strategy of playing things down rather than building them up, Pep spoke calmly on every subject. He assured people that Messi hadn't intended to hit anyone, but in order to avoid any misunderstandings he also apologised to anyone who felt offended. He cut short any discussions about Mourinho's tactics at the Bernabéu, maintaining that he never feels it appropriate to talk about the opposition's decisions. He took Di Stéfano's article light-heartedly, raising his hands and smiling, 'Whatever he's written, you'll never convince me that Don Alfredo has become a Barcelonista.' He made it clear that the reserve goalkeeper Pinto would play in the final, as he had in the previous rounds, instead of the first choice Victor Valdes: 'Pinto and 10 others', as if to say that keeping his word with his players was more important than the game. When he speaks first, Guardiola, as if in a judo contest, carefully avoids letting Mourinho use his weight against him to bring him down; he treads lightly, picking his way through thorny issues and keeping a cool head, because his rival is much better than he is at heating things up. Only the intrinsic tension of this sort of match, particularly in a series of four Clásicos one after another, could cause him to somehow be brought to earth. And Mourinho is an absolute master at finding any sort of handhold. Some may remember a scene from the great film *The Usual Suspects* where Kevin Spacey – who plays Keyser Soze – is being interviewed in a police station, and, by using his surroundings, is able to invent a very complicated story that diverts the police's attention away from himself. That day in Valencia, José was more like Keyser Soze than ever: as he caught the eyes of two journalists who had come from Italy – I was one, the other was Andrea Sorrentino from *La Repubblica* – his moment of inspiration came to create a story to bring him leaping out of the doldrums.

'They wrote that this isn't Inter!' Who knows if that's true, for a start. Di Stéfano didn't write that, nor did any of the three or four major Spanish newspapers that you have to read every morning, but since there are numerous daily papers and José receives a supposedly complete press review with his breakfast, we should take his word for it. Moreover, it's perfectly plausible given the perception that people have of Italian teams and of *calcio* in Madrid. If it isn't true, it's still believable.

'They wrote that Real Madrid aren't Inter because you can't just be satisfied with the result here, you have to constantly play on the attack to get it,' he declaimed in a mix of Italian and Spanish, even though all the Italians in a football press room can speak Spanish and vice versa. Every few words José directed his gaze towards us, and when he does he gives us the faintest of smiles. He has made that strategy his own: going on the attack against journalists from the country he's working in, based on the relationship he has with those he has previously worked with in other countries. If it's a good rapport, fine, otherwise he's capable of creating a positive one out of nothing. 'Ask Inter fans if they feel embarrassed at running out of room to sew the badges of trophies they've won onto their shirts,' and as he said this he pointed us out to our Spanish colleagues, satisfied that he had set out the premise for football's first media war. Indeed, his question – entirely rhetorical – didn't produce many smiles among the ranks of the Madrid press. But he now had the momentum, and the tension was starting to ease. You could almost hear the sparks. 'People tell me that Real Madrid must always behave with dignity, but I find that defending the name of the club, both on and off the pitch, is entirely part of this concept of dignity.' This barb had two targets: the first was Di Stéfano, who in his analysis had called for Real Madrid to reclaim a nobility that Mourinho didn't know how to embrace. He was here to win exactly like he had at Inter, at Chelsea before that, and at Porto before that. The idea that Real Madrid was different to Inter, and that there was a tradition – a tradition? – that for merely aesthetic reasons prevented him from simply playing the team most suited to winning with the available players, seemed completely alien to him. But the real target was the high priest of this philosophy: Jorge Valdano, Real's general director. It was apparent to everyone that he and Mourinho were never able to get along, most of all to Valdano, who had long confided to his inner circle that the Portuguese coach was never going to win over Florentino Pérez, who had returned to the club in 2009 after Ramon Calderon's presidency. 'The president doesn't believe that the coach is a dominant figure, on the contrary, he thinks he is a bit-part figure, caught between the strength of the club and the strength of the players.' As a result, after being turned down by Arsène Wenger, his first choice, who preferred to stay at Arsenal, Valdano turned to the 'engineer' Manuel Pellegrini, the elegant and affable Chilean whose sides played good football and who was ready for the step up after taking Villarreal to the semi-final of the Champions League. Even he, however, when coming up against the incredible technical ability of Barcelona, was forced to wave the white flag both at the Camp Nou and the Bernabéu, despite conducting the most expensive transfer window in history after bringing in Cristiano Ronaldo, Kaká, Karim Benzema, Xabi Alonso, Raúl Albiol and Álvaro Arbeloa. There had been too much money invested with nothing to show for it, too many losses to the Catalans – which is a problem in Madrid, and not just for sporting reasons. The temptation became too strong to hire a coach who had been able to eliminate Barça in the Champions League semi-finals while in charge of a technically inferior team, but who were nonetheless tough to break down and highly motivated, thereby preventing Real from enduring the ridicule of seeing the Catalans win the competition at the Bernabéu, where the final was to be played. 'I can no longer rule out Mourinho joining us, the injuries Guardiola inflicts on us every game somehow have to be cured, and he has shown he knows how to do it.' Jorge had just revealed this to his close confidants when Mou, who was coming off the back of his second Champions League win, this time with Inter, was spirited away into the Madrid night in Pérez's car, emerging the next morning having come to an agreement. It was already very clear to him though that Valdano wasn't a director who he would be able to work with, but was an enemy to be taken down as quickly as possible.

●

ZLATAN IBRAHIMOVIC, A MASTER OF USING slightly more succinct words but who has opinions that are no less clear and direct, once thought he had insulted Guardiola by labelling him as a 'philosopher'. He is not the first to misrepresent a profession, think of the contempt the Catalans have for Mourinho when they call him the 'translator'. The 'philosopher', in Ibra's denigratory interpretation, is a man who wastes time by thinking, someone who, like Icarus, dreams of flying high out of pure snobbishness while normal people, footballers included, carry out their lives with their feet on the ground. He had no time for this intellectual masturbation and instead behaved miserably, pursuing his own personal advantage as many others are wont to do. If it's possible, Valdano is even more of a philosopher – without inverted commas – than Guardiola, because the way in which he combines the technical side of football with the emotional intelligence he demands (of everyone: players, directors, fans) is relentless. And so Mourinho needed to beat him, and with him his vision, for the same reasons that caused Venerable Jorge in *The Name of the Rose* to kill the other monks who had, by reading the second book of Aristotle's *Poetics*, learned about comedy, laughter and their destructive influence on the principles of authority and dogma. Mourinho had set out his plans well before he received the call from Pérez: Valdano, with his high and noble philosophy, certainly had doubts about the ethics of the path the Portuguese had followed. But because Mourinho was able to build a winning team within the expected timeframe, Valdano was eventually ousted in a climate of complete derision. The attack against him in Real Madrid's (slightly pretentious) statement that announced his sacking – a display of ruthlessness reminiscent of the old *stile Juve* – was effectively a declaration of failure in Valdano. The common opinion was that results would be the deciding factor at the end of the season, but in reality the die was already cast, and it favoured the coach.

But where did Madrid's sudden desire to have a demiurge on the bench come from, given that Florentino Pérez's had always previously favoured signing star players – regardless of whether they could realistically all play together on the pitch – rather than coaches? The answer was contained in Valdano's logic: given that Guardiola was such a merciless rival that he wounded Madrid more and more every game, they needed the ideal anti-Guardiola to stop him. We'll never know if Pérez ever tried to hire the Blaugrana coach himself, in the same way that he discreetly tried to sign Messi without success. But it's likely that the Real president's attempts would have been stopped by Pep's uninhibited Catalan nationalism, forcing him to find a cure for the problem instead, a cure that he soon found in the Portuguese coach when he saw how he negotiated the Champions League semi-final in his second season with Inter. In charge of an undoubtedly strong team, though not as good as Barça, Mourinho shifted the pressure onto the Catalans with supreme skill, accusing them of being obsessed with the chance to win the trophy at the Bernabéu, thereby giving a negative, almost sick connotation to what was a simple desire for glory in a forbidden temple. Whenever Barcelona reach the Copa del Rey final and aren't playing Real Madrid, there is always the same obvious debate about where the game should be played. Logic suggests the Bernabéu – second in Spain only to the Camp Nou in terms of capacity – but there's always something to make that impossible: either Real are doing work on the stadium, or the security staff are on strike, or the turf is being relaid. In short, Barcelona had been unable to celebrate at the Bernabéu, and therefore, in Mourinho's words, being able to do so had become an obsession for the Blaugrana.

After giving himself the psychological advantage, Mou also won the tactical battle by dominating the first leg (3-1 in San Siro) and holding out with 10 men in the return leg in the Camp Nou (1-0 to Barça). Barcelona's poor performance, despite being at the peak of their powers, was partly due to some unfavourable circumstances, such as being forced to travel to Milan in a coach after the Icelandic volcano Eyjafjallajökull erupted, causing flights across the majority of the continent to be suspended due to the ash cloud covering vast swathes of European air space. Be that as it may, Mourinho managed the semi-final (and then the final against Bayern Munich) perfectly, and his spell at Inter went some way to restoring his reputation as a man of providence, or the Special One, after it had been somewhat tarnished by his first sacking by Chelsea. Mourinho had first been sounded out for the job when he went for dinner in Paris with Massimo Moratti two years earlier, the day after Inter had been knocked out of the Champions League Round of 16 by Liverpool, and the Nerazzurri owner was feeling particularly bitter as a result of Roberto Mancini's defeatist outburst (Following that 3-0 aggregate loss to Liverpool, Mancini claimed he was to quit as Inter manager at the end of the campaign, only to change his mind). He didn't say yes straight away, because at the time he was still hoping to succeed Frank Rijkaard on the Barça bench. But he could see how determined Moratti was to hire him and how much he wanted to make Mancini's winning team on the domestic scene into an even better one over the next two years. After not making a particular impression in the transfer market in his first season, at the start of his second year he then put his faith in two La Liga rejects' desires for revenge: Wesley Sneijder, sacrificed by Real to make way for more new arrivals, and Samuel Eto'o, who Barcelona used as a makeweight in order to sign Ibrahimović from Inter. Pep had been trying to sell the African forward, who had scored in Champions League finals both under Rijkaard and Guardiola, for some time: he had asked for him to be sold as soon as he took the Barça job, as he also did with Ronaldinho and Deco, but president Joan Laporta practically forced him to keep him, and ultimately no one regretted the decision. But even after a positive first season, Guardiola once again asked for Eto'o to be sold as it was difficult to manage his overly competitive spirit: the Cameroonian was the sort of person who urged his team-mates to work increasingly hard during training sessions, which coaches generally appreciate at the start but find it hard to support in the long run, because it is for them to decide when to reprimand, not the players, regardless of how charismatic they may be. If you know your full-back has hardly slept the night before because his newborn baby is teething, you can let him have a short rest. If his team-mate hits out at him for being too lazy, however, there comes a time when you have to tell him to be quiet, even if he appears to be in the right. The problem was a perennial one with Eto'o, until Pep – his mouth watering at the opportunity of signing Ibra – decided upon this disastrous choice. And so it was partly by counting on Eto'o's understandable desire for revenge that Mourinho moulded his treble-winning Inter side. Florentino couldn't have asked for more.

●

THE ROWS OF PEELING DESKS IN THE MESTALLA

press room are reminiscent of an old classroom, with journalists sitting below the raised platform from which so many lectures have been given. Mourinho couldn't have looked more like an old-fashioned teacher if had a cane in his hand with which to threaten reprobate journalists. The best of my Madrid-based colleagues, Diego Torres of *El País*, always had a dreamy expression on his face when he looked at him: he hated him – and would later write a savage but well-informed book about Mou's three years at Real – but he couldn't live without him. He, and others, had the same attitude as many of Howard Stern's listeners, the New York DJ who presented an irreverent and provocative radio show – a bit like *La Zanzara* – which had resounding success for many years at the turn of the century. A sizeable number of his listeners claimed to hate him, but continued to listen out of curiosity to see just how far he would have the nerve to go. This is one of the most significant aspects of Mourinho's dialectics: the certainty that he can keep pushing the boundaries of any debate, whether in a press conference or an interview.

There were certainly also some who were on his side within the large number of reporters who follow Real Madrid, although he did make an interesting and scathing comment about them to the two Italians present: 'I went for lunch with Ettore Messina. He thinks that the Madrid press always hopes that Real don't win, and I have to agree with him.' Some years later the great basketball coach confirmed this to me, albeit in a less cutting manner as his linguistic style is much more akin to Guardiola's, but added that he held the Portuguese coach in great esteem. 'If I think about the pressure that I had to put up with when I was the coach of Real's basketball team, and then about what he had endure as their football team's coach, which is a thousand times worse, I can only admire his resilience.' But are there really journalists who hope the team that sells their newspapers or makes people turn on their televisions fails? For a small club the answer is no, because every victory brings their journalists new columns, new journeys, new popularity. But it's slightly different for a big club, as the journalists who report on them are usually better, those who travel regardless of results (those who follow Real often also report on the Spanish national team, a bit like in Italy for those who report on Juventus) and who only need to demonstrate their skill when the atmosphere turns sour. When a team wins, everyone praises the club and the team, and the celebratory mood softens the differences between everyone's articles. When a team loses, however, journalists' content reflects controversy, anger and the issues behind the scenes, and it becomes easy to distinguish who has what agenda in the newspapers. In short, people work harder but they can also get themselves noticed; after all, no one who doesn't have an ego has ever become a journalist. What happened in Madrid probably went something like this: after meeting Messina, Mourinho tucked his comments away in his mind, and at the right juncture used them as a stick to beat the journalists with. He was so determined to teach the Madrid press a lesson that he even rejected an easy anti-Catalan diatribe when they asked him for his opinion on the comments apparently made by Piqué after the previous game. Shortly before, they had also asked the same question of Guardiola, who took care to play it down. 'I've asked Gerard if he really said that, and he assured me he didn't.' It may be that Pep wanted to protect his player, it may be that he honestly believed him, but the defender's separatist beliefs that he would later proclaim inevitably strengthened the narrative. Mourinho, however, paid it no attention. 'I come from a small country which is full of problems, but at least we all get along with each other.' A good answer. And the team, José? 'Sergio Ramos and 10 others.' A reference to Guardiola's answer about Pinto, but by naming the Real captain he was hinting at the exact opposite. He would be playing his strongest possible team.

THREE

PRIOR TO BECOMING JOHAN CRUYFF'S ASSISTANT
on the club's coaching staff, Carles Rexach was a talented forward for the Blaugrana. But history will always remember him as the man who signed the 13-year-old Lionel Messi after watching him play in a youth game. It is said that it took him just 50 paces to make up his mind. The story goes that the young Leo was taking part in a trial at the Mini Estadi when Rexach – who was scouting for young players for the future at the time – came out of the dressing room door, level with the halfway line. The other scouts were on the other side of the pitch with all their paraphernalia (lists, line-ups, identifications, pens), and since the game had already started Charly was forced to walk the long way round behind one of the goals. He kept an eye on the pitch as he

walked round the near side, and Rexach claims to have realised what a phenomenon this boy would turn out to be before he had reached the corner flag – 50 paces, more or less. Once he reached his colleagues he ordered the young boy to be taken off the pitch immediately, just in case. Maybe he was concerned that another club's scout was hidden among the small crowd of parents sat watching in the stands...It should also be added that Leo's father, Jorge, had already prepared a video with clips of his son doing tricks, which included a display using an orange which was reminiscent – who knows how consciously – of the talent of a young Diego Maradona. Either way, Rexach only needed those 50 paces to realise that what he had seen in the video wasn't just the usual compilation of clips cleverly put together, but the absolute truth.

Rexach is also famous for his equation, which all Barcelona coaches are required to know: only 30% of a Blaugrana coach's work is done on the pitch and with the team. The other 70% consists of controlling the media, political and managerial worlds that revolve around the team. The *Entorno*, to use one of Johan Cruyff's famous definitions.

Guardiola has always agreed with Rexach's equation about the *Entorno*, hinting at how uneasy he was with using up so much of his energy on something that, at the time, left him feeling heavily drained. Attempting to dig deeper into his relationship with the *Entorno* was made more difficult because of the distance that he always maintained between himself and the media , because while Mou tends to meet expectations and provide content in pre-match press conferences, Pep's strength is in avoiding doing so, or, rather, to tread lightly through them – soundlessly if possible – to avoid waking the atmosphere's demons.

We're now in the final stages of Pep's third season on the bench, and right from the start he said that he could only imagine himself there for a finite period of time, proved by only signing one-year contracts and in allowing a bit of suspense to build before he would sit down to discuss a new deal. In fact, in his first year, before he had even won anything, Guardiola was practically forced into a renewal on the night of his birthday, 18 January. He and his wife Cristina went to celebrate by going to a Manel concert, a very popular Catalan band, and when the lights went up after the final encore the 600 spectators and the musicians on the stage sang happy birthday to him, complete with a request for him to sign the contract they were yearning for. Won over by this affection, Pep went to see president Laporta the next day to extend his deal for another year. He only ever accepted yearly contracts in Catalonia, while at Bayern – who made the biggest investment in a coach ever seen in Bavaria for him – he signed (and respected) a three-year contract. He then agreed the same length of contract with Manchester City.

Seventy per-cent of Guardiola's energy needed to be used up on 'politics', and during the series of four Clásicos Laporta was a big concern for him in this regard. It was his vote to appoint him as first team coach that had swung the balance away from Mourinho, whose candidature had been put forward by other members of the board, but the president had come to the end of his term the previous summer and had had to step down. Sandro Rosell was elected as his successor, and while he was said to have been a close friend of Guardiola he was now somewhat obliged to support him: every president wants to choose his own coach (and his preferred choice was Luiz Felipe Scolari), but when he was elected Pep was already under contract, so he could only show, or at least feign, enthusiasm. Guardiola had already agreed a second renewal during the final months of Laporta's presidency. But, with his usual propriety, he waited for Rosell's appointment – and his clear approval – before putting pen to paper. The rapport between the two presidents, however, was not good at all, and even resulted in the new incumbent of the Camp Nou presidential box instigating legal proceedings against the former president for a series of financial excesses. True, these included reinforcing the doors of his own home, but if you consider that Laporta banned the most violent group of supporters from the stadium then you can understand him taking precautions. Guardiola suffered acutely from the diatribe between the old and new presidents, which was partly because Laporta had become a friend, and when the two went to dinner he would hear endlessly, frankly and tearfully about the uncertainty of his financial situation (the lawsuit was eventually dropped, but at the time there was talk about confiscating all his assets). Pep remained deeply unsettled, to the point where he pushed for a question about the topic in a press conference so that he could say 'I am deeply concerned about what is happening to President Laporta.' Naturally this made Rosell furious, but he was unable to say anything to his untouchable coach. Two months before the quadruple header against Real Madrid – which needed to be confronted with all other questions answered or set aside – Guardiola had renewed his contract with Barça for a third time, and he was aware deep down that it would very probably be for the last time.

The methods Pep uses and the intensity with which he applies them aren't sustainable indefinitely. Paradoxically, the job on the pitch – meticulous, painstaking work designed to ensure every player has at least three options when he receives the ball – is mentally the most relaxing aspect of it. The real stress comes from studying videos. Guardiola spends hours and hours studying opponents, because he wants to watch all their matches in order that he can be sure that a particular action always corresponds with a particular reaction. After a while Barcelona gave him a brilliant team of analysts; a couple of times I happened to be sat near them in the press box – they always work in pairs: one 'scans' Barça, the other the opposition – and of course I took a peek at some of the information they were gathering. It was an impressive array of statistics. But Guardiola only gives them a quick glance to find out a team's rough pattern of play, and then he watches the game again regardless. Nothing in a game escapes him, but it comes at the cost of working from 9 in the morning until 9 in the evening, and the only concession he gives himself – during the countless hours of watching videos – is having some classical music on in the background.

Working alongside him in the new training ground at Sant Joan Despí is one of Pep's old friends, who he wanted to have as an advisor, an assistant, a team manager, and an intermediary between him and the squad. He's a slightly special jack of all trades, because Manuel (Manel, in Catalan) Estiarte is considered – like our own Eraldo Pizzo – to be the greatest water polo player ever, so much so that he has been called his sport's Maradona. I was introduced to Estiarte by Marcos Lopez, a journalist working for *El Periódico* and a close friend, the first time I went to the press room in the Camp Nou when Guardiola was in charge. It was on 14 September, 2008 – the previous night, Barça had played their second league game of the season at home to Racing Santander, and after an away defeat against Numancia in the first game, they could only manage a draw, despite what was widely regarded to be an outstanding performance. One point from two games was a poor return even for a high profile but inexperienced coach like Pep, and in the press room there was a certain amount of nerves: there were only two days to go until the Champions League group stage started – I was staying to cover it – and he couldn't afford to get it wrong. But while everyone was wondering whether Guardiola had realised that the time for experimenting was over, the coach continued to rotate his squad and even promoted two players, Sergio Busquets and Pedro, from the Barcelona B team, who he had coached the previous season.

At that time we couldn't possibly be aware that Guardiola was different to other coaches in terms of how he evaluated players. Arrigo Sacchi developed a Leninist style of football in the shadow of Silvio Berlusconi at AC Milan, an extraordinary paradox and never sufficiently explored, and by taking his methods to extremes, Pep showed he is also a theorist of permanent revolution, a political legacy of Vladimir Ilyich. There is no formation that cannot be improved: once a team has tried a particular move it has already become obsolete, because a good opponent has already started to look for a counter-measure. Revolutions must be continual, partly in order to prevent players from resting on their laurels; while this would only be natural after a lot of victories, it would also inevitably lead to defeat. These are concepts that we would come to recognise, but which were still distant and mysterious after the first two disappointing results. The night before, however, I had guessed right with my article by writing that, the draw notwithstanding, Barça would go far with the style of football they had played. It was a stroke of luck (people write a lot of nonsense, particularly when a coach is just starting out, but instant judgements are necessary) that immediately paid off: Marcos introduced me to Estiarte, explaining that he was also responsible for relations with the international press. There was an immediate bond between Manel and I, and after chatting for 10 minutes, he said, 'Let me take you to Pep, he wants to meet you.' Maybe those 10 minutes were a test.

Guardiola hadn't yet confirmed his practice of never allowing individual interviews, but there was still the strong feeling of being allowed a great privilege. Manel took me behind the staging area into a corridor onto which open a number of the club's operational offices; the real headquarters is in another building in the Camp Nou complex, the one next to the Palau Blaugrana. The coach's office is one of the last ones, and is the only one not to have a glass window. It's the most private. When I went in, Guardiola was sat at his desk, looking over some documents. As soon as he noticed me he quickly got up and came towards me with his hand outstretched. 'It's nice to meet you, Paolo, thank you for what you wrote today.' Of course, I was amazed. Estiarte, standing behind me, could sense my surprise, and, chuckling, explained: 'I go to buy *La Gazzetta dello Sport* every morning. Ever since he played in Italy, Pep has got used to reading it...' The coach nodded with a conspiratorial smile. I can't pretend that I didn't feel proud. I spoke with Guardiola for a few minutes, he showed me a wall adorned with various decoders, there were two televisions but it was easy to imagine he would need more space. 'Soon our new training facility at Sant Joan Despí will be ready.' This wasn't great news for a journalist: Barcelona had always trained at La Masia, the pitch next to the stadium and also the wonderful home of the club's youth academy. It's a comfortable walk from the Avenida Diagonal, the one that has numerous hotels, to get there. Sant Joan Despí is in the distant suburbs, at least 20 minutes away by taxi, a suburb of warehouses and supermarkets. I had been there once before for a semi-private event with Ronaldinho, organised by a sponsor (20 of us from around the world attended, and were allowed three questions each).

Guardiola appreciated the fact that *La Gazzetta* had given him time, recognising the signs of greatness in his team's play, despite the fact that the early results weren't encouraging. 'You had courage,' he said, though it's always necessary to maintain a balance between being grateful for and suspicious of compliments, a balance that should be in any journalist's DNA. 'So let's do an interview!' I made the suggestion directly, because there couldn't have been a better time to try, and in truth I didn't know if I would even get another opportunity. 'I don't do them, Paolo.' Guardiola had, almost imperceptibly, tensed up. 'I'll never miss a press conference and I won't put limits on them: if people ask me questions for two hours, I'll stay there for two hours. But no exclusives, because I can't give them to everyone and I don't want to choose: you're all equal in my eyes, even though I know very well that that isn't the case.'

●

BEFORE RETURNING TO VALENCIA AND THE EVE

of the Copa del Rey final, it's worth taking a closer look at Estiarte, who has continued to be in Pep's shadow for the last eight years. The two have known each other for a long time. Not quite from childhood, given that Manel is 10 years older, but their status as icons of Catalan sport ensured they soon got to know each other. Estiarte is from Manresa, a town in the hills above Barcelona, while Guardiola was born and raised a few kilometres away in Santpedor, a village in the countryside. In the opposite direction, going towards the city, you find Terrassa, the hometown of Xavi, to complete the Blaugrana nativity scene. Estiarte has always been like a big brother to Pep. At the 1992 Olympics, a key moment in the recent history of Barcelona, the former was Spain's water polo captain and the latter was in the football team. It was no triviality for two fierce Catalans – Guardiola is proudly separatist, Estiarte has made his own position less clear – who were also proud to lead two extremely competitive groups of men. Pep won the gold medal, his only success with Spain. Manel...well, the final that he lost in the Bernat Picornell swimming pool on the hill of Montjuïc on the final day of the Olympics was a huge disappointment, but was also one of the most exciting chapters in Italian sporting history. Yes, because it was Italy who ultimately beat them in a timeless, wonderful match, which was decided by a goal from Nando Gandolfi in the sixth period of extra time. Just four years later though, in Atlanta, Manel was able to achieve his dream of winning the title: overall, he took part in six Olympic Games, from Moscow in 1980 to Sydney in 2000, and is the only Spaniard (in any sport) to have done so. The Maradona of water polo indeed.

Guardiola needed a figure with this level of prestige to keep his lines of communication open. He was like an ambassador: with the club, with the press (particularly international), and with his own players, who would accept any kind of advice, both psychological and behavioural, from a man with Estiarte's charisma, given that Manel knows his limitations and – unless it is with Guardiola in the confines of his office – doesn't risk intruding on the technical side of things. To understand the subtlety of his personality, and his success in a complex environment like the Barcelona dressing room, it's worth citing the first chapter of *Todos Mis Hermanos*, Estiarte's brutally honest and exhaustive autobiography, and which unfortunately no publishers have yet thought to translate into Italian. A real shame, such profound books about sport are anything but common. Other than recounting his successes, in fact, Manel deals with two huge tragedies that left their mark on him, the two suicides of his sister Rosa and of Jesus Rollan, the great Spanish water polo goalkeeper, as the result of depression. I read an advance copy of the book, and those chapters are like taking punches to the gut: I know that Guardiola's face was streaked with tears when he read it, but he didn't want to put the book down before finishing it.

The way that a person with this background describes a sporting failure is equally extraordinary. In his opinion, Spain began to lose the '92 final against Italy just before the start, when a hold up in the pre-game ceremony – a few members of the royal family had turned up to watch – forced the teams to wait in the long, dark tunnel that connected the changing rooms to the swimming pool. No one spoke, the tension was palpable. Estiarte recalls that the only sound was the players' feet on the tiles. He played in Italy, for Pescara, and knew the Azzurri team perfectly, some were his club team-mates, and in the darkness he prayed that none of his team-mates broke that magical silence; as the captain, before they had left the dressing room he had instructed them not to do so in their final team talk. He feared that any word could give their opponents an added incentive. But their nerves were like a cat in a bag, and in the end something *had* to come out. '*Vamos a ganar contra estos comepizza.*' It isn't a bad insult, 'we're going to win against these pizza eaters' is no big deal, but Estiarte felt himself die inside. 'Campagna and Ferretti, who were looking ahead, turned their eyes towards my team-mate. They didn't say a word, they just gave him a deadly stare. I knew about both of their characters, and of the other Italians. I knew that we had just given them added motivation.' Estiarte was right. At the end of a legendary final, when the players' energy was completely sapped and they were running on nerves and ambition, the player who scored the last and crucial goal to make it 9-8 was an Italian. A man who can tell similar stories with such perception should feel completely at home sat on the bench in the dressing room next to people like Carles Puyol and Xavi; of course I don't mean that he will explain the world to them, but the players will at least listen to him attentively. Armed with an advisor that everyone knows is very close to him, but who has such a strong personality and who is acknowledged not just to be simply an informer to the coach, Guardiola ruled the dressing room by learning what a coach needed to know, but also gave Estiarte the discretion to act on the secrets that people confided in him as he saw fit.

FOUR

AT 9.30 ON 20 APRIL, 2011, THE NAVARRESE REFEREE
Alberto Undiano Mallenco, considered to be Spain's best, blew
his whistle to get the Copa del Rey final underway. The Mestalla
is a stadium that is always noisy, its steep stands full of supporters who are more than capable of making themselves heard.
That evening the people of Valencia obviously stayed at home,
leaving their theatre to be invaded by Blancos and Blaugrana;
and so, in the narrow square off the main stand, thousands and
thousands of Real and Barça fans mingled as they waited for the
team coaches to arrive. On the fringes of the square, there were
a dozen excellent bars serving tapas, the classic and tasty traditional Spanish appetizers; in short, the two sets of fans mixed
in an essentially convivial atmosphere, but it also has to be said

that there is nowhere nicer to be in before a La Liga game than the Mestalla. None of this would ever happen at the Bernabéu or the Camp Nou, because the amount of tickets sold to away fans is so low that they are confined to spending the build up to the game far from the ground. While there was still a chance of incidents occurring here, the Valencia climate is charming, and not just because it's always sunny. Half an hour before the start, King Juan Carlos arrived with Queen Sofía. All the directors were lined up waiting for his entrance, and he greeted the heads of the ceremony, shaking hands with a stiff Florentino Pérez and surprisingly gave Sandro Rosell a little royal slap, who smiled at the friendly gesture. There is always a lot of talk about geopolitical issues before these games, we know that many Catalans want independence, and the meaning they assign to Barça's successes is clear. Just think about Piqué's quip of a few days previously: 'Little Spaniards, on Wednesday we're coming to Valencia to win your King's cup.' Or as the great Manuel Vázquez Montalbán described his beloved side: 'The unarmed army of Catalonia.' Juan Carlos played it down, but even so he wasn't spared a barrage of whistles when he took his seat in the stadium and even afterwards, during the national anthem. It was a warm spring evening, and the Mestalla was a bubble of colour and passion in the humid Mediterranean climate.

Real Madrid were overwhelming at the start. They pressed very high when Barcelona had the ball in their defensive third, in order to win it back in a dangerous area and try to strike quickly. After having used him four days before at the Bernabéu for just under an hour, Guardiola had dropped Carles Puyol, who was sat on the bench with an ice pack on his knee. The captain's final years of his career – he would retire in 2014 – were marked by a number of injuries that forced him to carefully manage the number of minutes he played. But with Javier Mascherano filling in for him, there was a marked drop in their ability to move the ball around in defence quickly and efficiently diminish. This didn't go unnoticed by Mourinho, who had named Pepe in midfield but instructed him not to advance beyond the opposition defence. 'You have to play much higher up than you did on Saturday, you have to press Mascherano and Piqué when they're trying to come forward, and when the ball goes out wide you have to support Özil on the right and Di María on the left. I'm asking you to do a lot of running, but if you succeed then this time we'll win.' Mourinho's setup was a more courageous 4-3-3 than usual, as he inverted the midfield trio from the first game by putting Pepe at the tip of the triangle (rather than the deep-lying midfielder he was before) and instructing the other central midfielders Sami Khedira and Xabi Alonso to play slightly deeper. It was an aggressive move that sought to take the initiative away from Barcelona, to undermine their calmness and to force them to work out how to counter it while the game was still going on, which they had almost never needed to do before, and so Mourinho was betting on the fact that the Catalans hadn't been preparing for the unexpected in training. The idea worked for the entire first half, because after the first few scares Guardiola ordered Busquets to stick tight to Pepe in order to reduce the impact he was having when pressing. By doing this, however, he sacrificed the Catalan midfield triangle's usual equilibrium: Xavi and Iniesta were forced to reconsider their positional play, and disorder – Barça's nemesis – reigned within the Blaugrana ranks. Watching a contest between a confused team unsuccessfully trying to play their usual possession game and a team playing with the frenzy of a mastiff barely restrained by its chain was spectacular in terms of excitement, but the quality was poor, partly because there was a dramatic rise in the number of fouls as a result. Within this cycle of Clásicos, what marked the Copa del Rey meeting out was that it was the first one in which even international team-mates put all friendships aside: in 2011, a number of these players had won both the European Championships (2008) and the World Cup (2010) together with Spain. Players like Casillas, Ramos and Xabi Alonso had shared this experience with the likes of Puyol, Xavi and Iniesta, but right from the off the duel between Alvaro Arbeloa and David Villa on the right hand side of the Madrid defence was incredibly punishing, while the Catalan midfielders would complain for a long time – albeit privately – of the abrasive and at times provocative attitude of Xabi Alonso. He clearly must have had a long talk with Mourinho, given that up until the previous game he was the main suspect for passing team news to the newspapers (which made the coach explode with anger in the dressing room) while from Valencia onwards his previously indifferent attitude towards José transformed itself into an almost military obedience. In reality the Portuguese, a master of psychological warfare, had been pushing the ideas of competition and false friendship for days. Marked by his previous, and certainly not short, experience in Catalonia, Mourinho had tried to convince his Spaniards to break off their friendships with their international team-mates at Barça, who were accused of claiming all the glory for La Roja's victories and of only feigning a great brotherhood with their Madrid compatriots.

'I know this atmosphere well, they're doing it for political reasons: they pretend that they're friends so that they can stab you in the back, don't be fooled by it.'

It would be a vulgar argument if it wasn't being put forward by a charismatic man like José; but the words that he used clearly made an impression, given that the viciousness of the tackles – quickly reciprocated by the opposition – soon reached dangerous levels.

Other than changing Pepe's position, Mourinho made some other important adjustments. Sergio Ramos was restored to central defence, in order to provide the power and ability to come forward with the ball that Albiol lacked. As we've already seen, Arbeloa had come in at right back, while up front he dropped Karim Benzema – who didn't impress him – and gave the role of centre forward to Cristiano Ronaldo, which was primarily to allow him to put Mesut Özil back into the side after a short spell on the sidelines. José's relationship with the German playmaker was somewhat complicated. He was certainly one of his men, he had wanted to sign him at any cost after being won over by his performances at the World Cup in South Africa, but he had been excluded from his inner circle because, his detractors – probably correctly – say, he wasn't part of the group of players managed by Jorge Mendes, Mourinho's own agent. Real was full of them, from Ronaldo to Carvalho, from Pepe to Di María. It has always been that way with the Setubal-born coach, from the Portuguese players he signed from Chelsea to when he forced Ricardo Quaresma on Inter. Unlike some of his team-mates, however, Özil didn't change his agent. And every time Mourinho kept him out of the starting line-up – even though he was very highly regarded by the rest of the squad – players would exchange long looks with each other across the dressing room, as if they thought that being picked for the team was about more than just technical ability. In any case, Özil was initially sacrificed on Saturday to add another defender to the midfield, but his introduction after an hour (for Benzema) significantly helped Real to equalise despite the fact they were down to 10 men. As a result, Mourinho, who had most likely given up on La Liga seeing as he retained most of his strength for the cup final, immediately selected him for the starting line-up in Valencia, again in place of the French centre forward. Cristiano Ronaldo was more than capable of playing as a number 9.

It was an excellent choice, because Özil, who was itching to play, played two perfect balls for the Portuguese superstar within the first half hour. The first was an expertly played clipped pass at the end of a rapid counter-attack led by Di Maria, but Cristiano's touch was slightly too loose and he was forced away from his central position, and his subsequent cut back from a wider position was intercepted by Mascherano; the second was a high ball played by the German with perfect timing to find Ronaldo in an onside position. As the Madrid fans looked bewildered at seeing him miss the ball – a rarity, considering who made the mistake – the Catalan supporters looked visibly relieved; throughout the first half, they believed it was inevitable that they would concede. Real's best chance came in the 44th minute, and it was a result of a magnificent right-footed cross from Özil, as usual, which found an unexpected centre-forward: Pepe himself, who rose above Dani Alves to meet it with a header, no more than eight metres from goal. His header came back off the post, and as they went back into the dressing room, Real's players had the concerned expressions of players who are too experienced not to know that in football, when you are the better team, you have to take your chances, because games can change and you never know if and when you will regret your missed opportunities.

Both coaches talked a lot during the half-time interval. Guardiola needed to correct his team's unusual attitude, which was almost submissive in the face of their opponents' tactical and physical aggression. Since he had taken charge, Barça had beaten Real five times before the draw on Saturday, and among those five wins was the incredible 2-6 in the Bernabéu in his first year and the extraordinary humiliation of the previous December, the 5-0 that will always haunt Madridistas. If they let this cup slip away by allowing Real to do what they wanted as they had in the first half, the psychological advantage that he had established would disappear, as their eternal rivals would realise that not even a team who had beaten them that easily was itself ultimately unbeatable. There's a cliché about love, but it can be applied, more or less, to football as well. It's a wonderful phrase in *Damage*, the masterful book by Josephine Hart (you must at least have seen the film, with Juliette Binoche and Jeremy Irons). It goes, 'damaged people are dangerous, because they know they can survive', and that is exactly how Real Madrid felt after the draw – playing with 10 against 11 – that Saturday. They had been seemingly irreparably damaged by the three years of Guardiola's Barça, yet they had still survived and maybe found the key to installing their own virus in the perfectly built software of the Catalans' game.

During the 15 minutes at half-time Pep didn't shout – he

almost never does – but he indicated the tactical and psycho-logical adjustments required to rid the team of its inertia in an extremely decisive tone. The team listened to him without breathing a single word.

In the other dressing room, José Mourinho was walking a tightrope. On the one hand he wanted to tell his players how much he approved of the way in which they had stifled Barcelona for 45 minutes – though while he approved, he was not satisfied, because they were still looking for the goal that should have af-firmed their dominance. On the other hand, he needed to tell his men that Barça would recover, probably at the very start of the second half. 'It's unthinkable that a team like them won't react, so I'm telling you to be prepared to struggle, it will be a long and difficult second half. Right now Guardiola, in the dressing room next door, is telling his players how to turn the tables on us: be ready to help each other, be tight and compact, there are areas where you will be targeted, and if they take you on one-on-one you'll be in trouble.' Al Pacino couldn't have said it better.

And the game did change. That was immediately obvious. Barcelona's midfield rediscovered its balance, Pepe's frantic press-ing slowed because his team-mates were no longer able to keep pace with him, and Xavi and the others began playing their pos-session game again, the closest thing to hypnosis ever seen on a football pitch. The Catalan fans' demeanour noticeably changed as well: while they had suffered in the first half, fearing a goal was coming, now they were holding their breath as they waited for their side to take the lead and seemed even more worried, be-cause the fear of not taking your own chances always exceeds that of giving chances to your opponent. The source of this worry is the fear of mockery, because conceding while the other team is on top is only natural, but conceding when you're in full control of the game is a sign of incipience. And in football, image is crucial. Fabio Capello, another top quality coach, abhorred the very idea of conceding a goal on the counter-attack, which is widely considered to be the intelligent answer to those unwary coaches who spend their lives excessively teaching attacking football.

Barcelona decisively attacked down the left hand side, where penetrating runs were made alternately by Pedro and Villa. In reality it was always Messi, who moved freely across the entire forward line, who directed the play, but the idea of attacking Marcelo, who operated down the right hand side (looking at the pitch from the Catalans' perspective), was less appealing to him than attacking the space behind Arbeloa, who was seen as the weak point of Mourinho's team. After a few attempts, with shots from Pedro and Villa failing to hit the target, in the 68th minute the moment seemed to have arrived. Messi picked up the ball just inside the Real Madrid half, and set off leaving Marcelo, Xabi Alonso and Khedira in his wake. Sergio Ramos closed him down to try and stop him before he could go any further, while Ricardo Carvalho stretched the defensive line by moving closer towards Arbeloa, who at right back was the last man. These were perfect movements, straight from a defensive coaching manual, but they didn't take the Argentine's almost supernatural speed into account. He slipped past Ramos' tackle, passing the ball into the smallest of gaps between Arbeloa and Carvalho. It was a fantastic ball to find Pedro in a goalscoring position after he had raced past Arbeloa on his blind side, and his low shot beat Casillas to send the Barça fans into raptures. As they celebrated though, they saw Undiano Mallenco had already raised his hand to indicate a free kick to Real Madrid. The linesman still had his flag raised, signifying that Pedro was offside. The furious Barcelona bench nearly spilled out onto the pitch, and Guardiola physically held back the most agitated – in the replays you can see Thiago Alcántara determined to exact justice – and honestly I have to say that, in the press box, the feeling was that a perfectly good goal had been ruled out.

We were wrong.

A few seconds later, the replay showed that the linesman, Fermin Martinez Ibanez, had made the call of his life: when Messi played his pass, Pedro's feet were in line with Arbeloa's, but, by leaning forwards, his chest and his head were offside. And so the offside decision, even if it was only just offside, was the correct decision. It's important to underline how close the call was and how fine the margins were, because during these 18 days Pedro's disallowed goal would take on the utmost importance. In fact, it was the spark that led to all out war. In that sense, it was a bit like the assassination of Archduke Franz Ferdinand in Sarajevo in 1914 that led to World War I.

But let us return to the Mestalla.

Barça's anger at the disallowed goal spurred them on, and in the final fifteen minutes they literally bombarded Real Madrid, forcing Casillas to make two stunning saves from Pedro, again, and from an apparently goal-bound shot from Iniesta. In his polite, understated way, Iker was the leader of the section of the dressing room that resisted Mourinho's crusade for provocation, the man who, backed by his beliefs, admitted that he was tired of the politics the Portuguese had brought to the rivalry, which used to be simply the best display of technical ability in Spanish, and often European, football. This was a stance that he would pay for by being dropped from the team before he had begun to decline as a player, which wasn't long in arriving, but had not yet arrived. After the game, Mourinho himself admitted that 'Casillas made two fantastic saves', but that would be the last compliment he would make publicly before freezing him out.

The save from Iniesta in the 80th minute, in particular, was made at full stretch, the tip of his finger brushing against the ball with just enough strength to turn it away from goal, and watching the replay from the camera positioned behind the goal you can see it was the difference between the ball finishing one side of the post or the other. Sergio Ramos, who had tried to stop the shot right up until the last moment, went up to his friend with an expression that was both grateful and incredulous at the miracle he had just witnessed. But at the Mestalla that night there was no time even to enjoy miracles as the game continued to ebb and flow. After the first half dominated by Real and the majority of the second half by Barça, the Madridistas came back again just before the full time whistle, the most deceptive of all periods of the game because every team tries to show they are willing to call a truce and settle for extra time, but beneath this cloak they are hiding a dagger with which they can strike the decisive blow when there's no time left to recover from conceding a goal. In the exciting final few minutes of the game, Real tried to strike that blow twice but missed both times: in the 87th minute Adebayor, who had replaced an exhausted Özil, led a break forward and found Ronaldo in an excellent position, but for once the Portuguese's control wasn't as fluid as it usually is.

It was too intricate, and it allowed Dani Alves the time to get back and close him down with a sliding tackle. Then, in the 89th minute, a wonderful piece of skill gave Di María space on the edge of the box: quick to step inside Alves, the Argentine struck a precise but soft right-footed shot towards goal, and although his dive certainly gave the final minutes a photogenic moment, given that it wasn't a particularly difficult save, Pinto showed that he wasn't just a cult hero: he turned the ball safely over the bar, and with it ensured that extra time would be necessary.

In the most finely balanced of contests, Guardiola and Mourinho were so busy implementing their moves and counter-moves that they had practically forgotten that they had substitutes: of the six possible changes, only Emmanuel Adebayor had come on for Özil when the Madrid playmaker had begun to feel the pace. One substitution for Mourinho, then, and none for Guardiola, who scrutinised the pitch as though the answer to the puzzle was hidden out there somewhere. Standing still, lost in his thoughts, for a long time Pep seemed to be in a catatonic state. Then he broke into action, approaching the crowd of players lying on the ground in need of a massage. On the other side of the halfway line, José had called everyone who worked for Real together, from the physios to the kit men. It might appear to be a way to deal with the atmosphere, but actually it was a strategy to prevent anyone from reading his lips to find out his instructions in advance: Barcelona may not appear to use a great deal of secret intelligence, but they do, and in abundance. A wall of people protected the conversation between Mourinho and his players, and with the benefit of surprise Real started the quicker out of the blocks. There were still no substitutions, but Pepe began pressing high up again while Adebayor, even though he wasn't the fine centre forward he used to be, gave his team more options as the depth he offered disturbed the fine balance that Barcelona thought they had only just restored. In an increasingly stretched midfield, the accuracy of Xabi Alonso's long balls once more began to have an effect, and, halfway through the first half of extra time, he picked out Ronaldo with a magnificent pass. The ball rolled past Piqué, but he could only watch it go by as Cristiano raced onto it: of the various individual duels theirs was the most exciting, because speed and power combined in equal measure, and they are two such imposing, giant figures that they could easily do an advert for *Clash of the Titans*. Moreover, the two knew each other well from their time playing together at Manchester United: it would perhaps be stretching things to call them friends, but there was always a visible mutual respect between them even during the most intensely competitive moments. So Ronaldo was rushing after Xabi's pass, with Piqué hopelessly far behind him. The Portuguese's right foot shot was struck with the force of a train cutting through the night, but once it passed Pinto's right hand, its trajectory imperceptibly changed, who knows how, and it brushed the outside of the post. A wonderful shot, but off target. Ronaldo stood there, disbelieving.

But that was only the warm up; the defining moment was about to arrive. In the 102nd minute, while Barcelona were once more unable to organise themselves in the face of their opponents' pressing, Pepe recovered the ball in midfield and gave it to Marcelo, who exchanged passes with Di María to set him free down the left hand side to cross. When the ball came into the Catalan penalty area, Piqué, the only Blaugrana player who was strong in the air, had left Ronaldo to go and mark Adebayor; Adriano, shorter and less agile, was picking up the Portuguese instead, and when the cross starts to drop just beyond the penalty spot, he realised that Ronaldo was already in the air, ready to meet his destiny. He hung in the air like a basketball player, he met the ball perfectly, heading it back across goal and taking Pinto by surprise, who desperately threw out a hand but to no avail. A wonderful goal. A goal that shattered the established order of a dominant Barcelona and a quivering Real Madrid. It was only a Copa del Rey final, but the Blancos celebrated with the passion of a team that has just won the World Cup. Pepe, the most malicious member of the team, couldn't resist the temptation to make a resounding umbrella gesture towards the Catalan fans sat in the stand behind the goal. Half-time quickly arrives. It should be a simple change of halves, but tiredness can kill, and a number of Madrid players collapsed to the ground near the bench: Mourinho had a word with each of them, putting an arm around Di María's shoulder, encouraging Arbeloa by telling him he only had to keep going for 15 more minutes, and replacing Khedira, who could no longer stand up, with the loyal Esteban Granero. At this point, Mou seemed like Russell Crowe in the opening scenes in *Gladiator*, the general moving among his troops in the midst of battle and supporting them with strong words of empathy.

Guardiola tried to change things, immediately putting on the Dutchman Ibrahim Afellay – what a wasted opportunity, incidentally – for the exhausted Villa, then Keita to give Busquets a rest, and finally Maxwell for Adriano. But none of his replacements led to anything, and ultimately from the moment that Ronaldo scored there was the feeling that his would be the only goal of the evening. The match was too tense, there were too many nerves on edge, too much agonised concentration. Barça still had eighteen minutes to turn the tide after going 0-1 down, but Madrid's defensive organisation didn't give them a chance. If anyone was still going to score it should have been Ronaldo in the 118th minute, but his shot was blocked by Dani Alves when the goal was gaping. A camera caught the annoyed reaction of Mourinho, who was already on his feet ready to celebrate the goal that would have made the game safe, but instead he was forced to endure two more minutes of passion (of sorts). But isn't that the sort of passion we all live for?

Final whistle.

Looking at each of the jubilant Madridista faces in turn, it's clear that Ronaldo was the most fired up, an unrestrained, total joy, free of any sort of constraint. Like all revelations, it's immediately apparent why this is: Ronaldo has just beaten Messi. It isn't the first time ever, Manchester United knocked Barcelona out in the Champions League semi-final in 2008, but that time Cristiano, by missing a penalty in the third minute of the first leg, was the man who put United's qualification at risk, and which was instead secured with a goal from the veteran Paul Scholes in the second leg. This time, however, he scored the only goal in a final – it would have been impossible to be any more decisive.

Ronaldo is a person who has a literary quality to his soul and a highly theatrical quality to his body. He completely rejects his status as the second best player in the world, as though it were a status of mediocrity, and accentuates his body language – the aforementioned theatricality – whenever he has the opportunity to do so, because it's there, in his athletic and elegant physique, that he finally feels superior to his rival, the proof of which is in the obvious preference of sponsors who are looking for a seductive face for their brand. As much as he has grown following his childhood hormone disorder, Messi has remained rather small, and there's little that's charming and nothing that's sexy about his appearance. He is, however, a football prodigy while Cristiano is 'just' a great player, and his dominance in that area – the area that is of most importance to both of them – has made the Portuguese Adonis into a beast. If Messi is Mozart, Ronaldo is no Salieri; he is much more than that. Not enough, however, to convince people that there is a competition for the world's best player: if you ask 100 supporters (neutral fans, not of one or the other) which of the two is better, it would be surprising if the ratio was less than 80:20. The real greatness of Ronaldo is in never having given up when faced with such an immovable obstacle (he has only won one La Liga title in seven seasons at Real, compared to his rival's five). There is something elusive in the Portuguese's determination to improve day after day, but that is exactly what makes him a great champion. Walter Di Salvio, his fitness coach at Manchester United (for years he secretly flew him and his treatment table out to Madrid, because the player thought what the Real staff were prescribing him was insufficient) once told me about the extra exercises – not his intense workout routines – Cristiano did after training at Carrington, United's training ground. While his team-mates went in for their showers, he went out to the back of the complex, where it borders on a patch of woodland, so that he could practice his ball control in difficult conditions. In the woodland undergrowth the terrain was very uneven, full of exposed tree roots, and Ronaldo would kick the ball hard into that area and chase after it, trying to bring the unpredictable bounces under control. When Walter told me about this, I immediately thought about the Brazilians and their technical ability, refined through hours of playing on the beach, and of the below average players in any league who can't wait for the end of every training session, and who don't do a minute more training than they are obliged to do. Everyone wants to become like Cristiano Ronaldo, but few know how hard he works to maintain his status. No one has described this contradiction to me as well as Gianluca Vialli once did: 'Every player will tell you that he has a great will to win, and that's true. But the ones who have the will to prepare themselves to win are those who make a difference.'

●

FROM THE STANDS IN THE MESTALLA, IT WAS clear to see what the final meant. After the final whistle sounded, the majority of the players – Real's embracing each other, Barça's in silence – collapsed to the ground and struggled to get back up, visibly exhausted. After using up so much physical energy, combined with the frightening mental pressure, the game demanded more than they had to give, and extra time had drained even their reserves. It was the scene of a pitched battle, and only two people from the Blaugrana ranks had the mental strength to cross the battle lines and congratulate the victors. The first was Madrid's enemy number one, the Catalan separatist par excellence, the most explicit secessionist: Gerard Piqué. Everyone in the city thinks that he will be Barcelona president one day because of his intelligence, preparedness, and his uniqueness among everything that surrounds him. His maternal grandfather Amador, whose surname somewhat ironically is Bernabéu, was director at the club for many years; his mother Montserrat is the director of the prestigious Institut Guttmann, a specialist centre for spinal injuries; his partner Shakira, mother of his two children, vies with Madonna and Lady Gaga for the accolade of the most famous music star on the planet. Being this sort of person, it's no surprise that, after taking a few moments to get his breath back and process the defeat, he walked purposefully towards the enemy camp to shake the hand of each member of the opposition. The same person who at the end of the first Clásico in the series, who was among the protagonists of the brawl in the tunnel; the same person who for political reasons even now struggles to speak to Sergio Ramos, his international team-mate. Piqué's gesture, greeted with surprise by some of the Madrid players, was the essence of sportsmanship. Or, as the cynics might say, simply empty rhetoric: Real were the better team, I gave my best but it wasn't enough, now I can only congratulate them.

Piqué aside, there was a lot of iciness on the pitch even between international team-mates: Arbeloa and Villa had fought throughout the match and now looked at each other menacingly even from a distance. Barcelona players – as mentioned earlier – would complain about Xabi Alonso's attitude for months afterwards. Including both those on the pitch and on the bench, there were in fact 12 World Cup-winning players, but there was no sign of the great Furia Roja squad.

After Piqué came Guardiola. The previous March, after miraculously surviving a Champions League tie against Juventus, Pep criticised the complaints made about the referee by

Bianconeri director Beppe Marotta: 'When a great club loses they mustn't look for excuses, but compliment those who beat them.' A noble idea, even if good grace suggests using it as little as possible; it is something, however, that Guardiola routinely does on nights where it is he who is beaten. Like this one. Or most recently, when Atletico Madrid knocked out his Bayern side, despite a stunning performance, to deny him his last chance at winning a Champions League in Bavaria: 'We should begin by congratulating Atletico', Guardiola had said.

Real Madrid's players went up into the stand, where the King of Spain was waiting for them with the trophy after the president of Catalonia had congratulated them with a handshake. There is a clear superiority in Pep in every aspect of his behaviour, including when he has been beaten; a moral superiority and a sense of feeling better educated which fascinates friends and admirers, but must be unbearable for those who are different or, in some senses, 'normal'. In this sense, and only in this sense, Mourinho is a normal person, because there's nothing zen-like in the anger he feels when he is beaten, it's a fury that would take the roof off the dressing room, and he doesn't give a fuck about shaking hands with opponents – sickening frippery for spineless losers.

The two pass each other only fleetingly, the handshake is brief, Guardiola is fairly calm in defeat while the victorious Mourinho's mind is still in turmoil.

A few players said privately that it was only at the airport, a couple of hours later, that the Portuguese coach seemed to be a bit more relaxed. He certainly wasn't when he arrived in the press room. Hunched over, almost hidden behind the small screen that was showing the game's highlights, Mourinho seemed exhausted.

In his interview, during which he skipped round questions like gates in a ski slalom to continue to talk about whatever he wanted to, the victory became almost incidental. 'This season we've played them three times: once we conceded five goals, we drew another and tonight we won. That means that anything can happen at any time between us. Naturally I'm happy to have won another domestic cup, which is my fourth: in addition to the cup in Portugal, my home country, I've won them in the three most important countries in European football: England, Italy and now Spain. But if we'd lost I would say the same things, because what mattered was the attitude of my players.' Don't be deceived by this slightly more modest attitude, coming from someone who had just exerted a huge amount of nervous energy. Mourinho had still mentally identified a few targets: one, incidentally, was the aforementioned Diego Torres of *El País*, who he had taunted from day one – 'I already know that some geniuses, for instance the gentleman sat in front of the computer in the third row there, will write pages and pages to explain this match'; but the primary target was Johan Cruyff, who had recently written in his column for *El Periódico* that the Portuguese was a 'titles coach' and not a 'football coach'. Mourinho had never explicitly talked about Barcelona (who he always referred to as *ellos*, them), as if he were trying to take away their dignity, let alone called Cruyff by name. But there was no question about who he was referring to. 'There is someone who recently said that I'm an *entrenador de titulos* and not an *entrenador de futbol*. Thank you. I like that. All of us here work hard so we can win titles, so I'll take that as a compliment.'

If the Madrid media had been almost unanimously sided

against him up until the day before, something noticeably began to change after the victory. Since Guardiola had taken charge, Barcelona had never lost against Real: five wins and a draw, the one that came four days before. The cup victory was confirmation that the tide was turning, and as much as Mou's methods clashed with the journalists following the team, beating this apparently unbeatable Barça team was the main priority, asking his people to do whatever it took to combat an unprecedented level of Catalan superiority. The man who had achieved that deserved unquestionable support, not to mention the fact that the fans, quicker than journalists, had already moved lock, stock and barrel to his side. José can feel the wind changing like few others, and if he allowed himself a quip against Torres it was because he knew that no one would come to his defence, they wouldn't risk causing another Karanka situation. He also made a very sarcastic comment on the Spanish media's obsession with ultra-attacking football: 'If I'd gone along with the newspapers I would have chosen a formation with six forwards, but I didn't change my mind and I think it went just fine.' The time had come to fan the flames a bit with a question about the monolithic, and very Catalan, way that football is viewed in Spain. He expected nothing less. He responded in Italian, but as you know everyone understood him. 'Here people think that good football is just about having possession. They're limited thinkers. I believe there are many other ways of playing well, like defensive organisation, solidarity, the ability to withstand pressure and to close down spaces while preparing a counter-attack at the same time. In my opinion tonight Real played a great match because they demonstrated all these qualities.' Aside from a small group of diehards, my Spanish colleagues were looking down at their shoes.

It was time for him to leave, but before he did José reminded Florentino Pérez about the most important promise that was now due to him. 'I'll go home happy with this win, but I would have been calm even if we had lost, because my job is going well regardless. I was promised that a few changes could be made to the club's structure to modernise it, and it seems to me that, little by little, I'm succeeding.' This final eviction notice to Jorge Valdano thus delivered, the president let it be known in the following days that he had received it. During the dinners that followed the victory – the celebrations went on in Madrid for days – he made no secret of his desire to keep Mourinho, and possibly offer him a contract extension, but he was also distancing himself from the man who for so many years had been his most loyal supporter, and whose relationship with the new coach now seemed irreparable.

●

THE TWO COACHES MISSED EACH OTHER IN THE press room by a matter of seconds, which suggested that a delay had been deliberately arranged so that they would avoid seeing each other. Guardiola and Estiarte came in together; the former sat at the table, the latter took up a sentry position in the opposite corner of the room. Elegant in his grey suit, which even after 120 minutes of tension looked as though it had only just been pressed, Pep initially looked vacant, with a bottle of water, his fourth or fifth of the evening, in his hand as always, and before every answer he took a swallow. 'First of all I want to congratulate Real Madrid.' The pre-programmed sportsmanlike statement. The diehards nodded their heads, the others puffed out their cheeks at what appeared to them to be a sudden display of ostentatious and slightly naive sportsmanship, or, as the Italians call it, *buonismo*. With this formality concluded, Pep gradually regained his colour as he nimbly and quickly extricated himself from unusual and unfamiliar questions about defeat. 'There isn't long left until the end of the season, it's time to reap what we've sown, so now we need to pick ourselves up quickly and start again. It would have been better to win, of course, and the result was in the balance for a long time: it could have gone either way, but it went their way, congratulations again to them. But my team didn't start out with me, they have experienced defeats before, and they've come back from them in the past. That's life, you get knocked down and you have to be capable of getting back up again.' It's possible that Guardiola was being coquettish when he said that this group of players hadn't started out under him and therefore they know the taste of defeat to Real Madrid, a situation which – as a coach – he had never been in until half an hour before. Perhaps he was being coquettish, perhaps it was a way of encouraging his players, or it was maybe a combination of both: 'courage, it's already happened now and you know how to carry on'. The most natural moment to bounce back would be that Saturday's La Liga game at home to Osasuna, and Pep even made mention of José Luis Mendilibar, the Pamplona side's coach who was held in high regard by the national media for his determination to play attacking football even when his team was vastly inferior to the opposition.

Real Madrid aren't the only club that are followed by a group of contrarian journalists. Some of those who follow Barça suggested that Guardiola was being a cry-baby by accusing Real of playing unfairly and, after half-time, very defensively. He looked at them like a weary professor; he had been teaching them a certain ethical style for three years and he was now being asked completely the opposite sort of question. 'I don't intend to use any arguments that could sound like I'm looking for an excuse. Every team decides how they want to play football, there's a referee to ensure the rules are respected, and that's all I intend to say on that. I'll finish this press conference as I started, by congratulating our opponents on their victory.' It was only a theoretical conclusion, because Graham Hunter, the compelling Scot who landed in Spain one day for the *Daily Mail* and never left, then asked the sharpest question of the evening. 'Do you not think that Leo Messi, in both Clásicos in the last few days, has played a bit too far away from goal?' Guardiola felt the pinch of that question because the observation was absolutely correct, and it was certainly his idea to play Messi deeper. 'Leo isn't just a finisher,' he said, in some ways happy to have finally been asked a worthy question, 'If I ask him to go and pick up the ball in a deeper position it's because I want him to be involved as much as possible in our game. You notice him when he gets involved.' A convincing reply, but Pep made a mental note to think further on Hunter's doubts.

FIVE

THE COPA DEL REY VICTORY BECAME A FORMIDABLE
weapon in Mourinho's arsenal, and in the following days he
consolidated his power both at Valdebebas, where he now had
complete control, and at the club's headquarters on the Con-
cha Espina. It settled the scores with Valdano, which had been
inevitable ever since January when the general director, after
biting his tongue for so long to present at least the façade of a
united front, let slip a comment on the squad's centre forwards.
Ever since the summer Mourinho had said that two number 9s,
Higuaín and Benzema, were insufficient; meanwhile the club,
who in addition to signing world class players always try to raise
some homegrown talent, had hesitated, convinced that the then
18-year-old Alvaro Morata would be able to fill the void if he

took his chances. After losing Gonzalo Higuaín to injury at the start of December, Mou went back on the offensive ahead of the January transfer window, which was partly because he lost some of his confidence in Karim Benzema due to his laziness in training. But the French forward was still the favourite of Florentino, who had gone to Lyon in person the year before to convince him to accept his offer. Aware of the president's favourable disposition towards the Frenchman, José never said anything directly against him, limiting himself to a number of sarcastic comments, such as at the start of December when he said, 'If I have a dog I go hunting with him and I'll come back with a full bag of game, if not I'll go hunting with a cat and somehow I'll make do, but I won't catch the same prey', where all the evidence pointed to Higuain being the dog and Benzema being the cat. But in mid-January, when he forced the situation at Almeria by dropping Karim and playing Ronaldo up front, Valdano fell into his trap by responding, without too much hesitation, to journalists' questions and feigning surprise. 'Why do we need another centre forward, if the ones we have are sent to sit on the bench?' It was the moment José had been waiting for. The next day he stormed into Florentino's office to accuse Valdano of interfering in his team selection, and after threatening to resign he ensured that the general director could no longer travel on flights with the team and that he was banned from entering the training ground at Valdebebas during training hours. Then, as a final flourish to appeal to the president's vanity, Mourinho suggested that Zinedine Zidane – another of Pérez's favourites – should inherit the director's responsibilities for the first team, which received his boss' enthusiastic approval. In the final days of the transfer window, the Togolese centre forward Emmanuel Adebayor was added to the squad on loan, allowing him to make good his escape from Manchester City: his physical decline had already started at just 27 years old, and in fact his contribution would be minimal. But for now Valdano was beaten and virtually removed from the scene, and the road towards complete control at the club – Mourinho's real obsession – was now open. Actually, it's worth understanding how much control it would be realistic for him to have in a complex environment like Real Madrid, which is profoundly different to the basic, hierarchical and ultimately patriarchal structures of Porto, Chelsea and Inter. At the clubs where he had been successful before, José had quickly and almost automatically become the sole person in command; the plenipotential owners (Pinto da Costa, Roman Abramovich, Massimo Moratti) followed only him and trusted only him. As much as Florentino Pérez cultivates similar compliance, Real is an institution that will never be about just one man, or at least not for a long period of time: it is more reminiscent of a medieval court than a great sports club, with its conspiracies, its traps, its corridors of power, its secrets, its traditions, the lovers that soon become fierce rivals, the stabs in the back from those who you thought to be friends. *House of Cards*, in short, and José would witness most of this during his decline and fall from grace in Madrid. But they were problems that would come later, because his victory in Valencia saw him reach the peak of his power.

We've already seen that the origin of the antipathy – to put it mildly – between Valdano and Mourinho was in their philosophical differences: they followed two opposing visions of football, and those who maintain that Jorge is a Barcelonista trapped in the body of a Madridista, whether it is a compliment or not, aren't wrong. Valdano, a prolific writer of both books and editorials for *Marca*, had never previously hesitated to criticise Mourinho, and since he isn't the sort of person who changes his mind, he admitted as much on the day the Portuguese coach was presented to the media. However, he underlined that his 'aggressive' remarks and Mou's equally 'aggressive' replies had been taken care of in a face to face meeting as is only natural for 'men of football'. Easy, no? A bit too easy. The Argentine's criticisms had run too deep, maintaining that every coach who hadn't been a great player in his day, or at least a good player, don't like being reminded of this (Sacchi is identical to Mourinho in this respect, but even so Valdano still holds him in high regard despite their ideas about football being polar opposites), and so their backward hunger for personal glory is precisely due to the frustrations of their youth at not being able to become a great footballer. Arrigo has long since answered this question with the same quip, 'You don't need to have been a horse to become a good jockey,' but it's an argument that weighs down on him. Mourinho had read that Valdano considers his desire for control to be a lack of faith in his players as a result of his inexperience: not having been a world class player, he doesn't know that world class players find the answer independently of their coach's tactical instructions. As critical observations go, that is not a flippant one. Taken literally, it would stop any player who hasn't been in the running for the Ballon d'Or from becoming a successful coach.

There's definitely something elitist in Valdano's theory, who after all was refined in the way he played and has a vastly more agile and profound mind than many other former top players.

While he was inspired by solid tactical principles and aided by excellent assistants like the Argentine Ángel Cappa – another very interesting character – Valdano's experience as a coach wasn't the success that everyone expected it to be: he won one La Liga title in 1995 – with a Real side containing Manuel Sanchís, Raúl, Fernando Hierro and Iván Zamorano – and nothing else. In fact, he was sacked in January the very next season by Lorenzo Sanz, Pérez's predecessor, who went on to appoint Fabio Capello in the summer. After a final unsuccessful spell at Valencia, Valdano had realised that his intellect was more suited to writing than to coaching, and Pérez's respect for him did the rest, bringing him back to Madrid in the role of general director both times he became club president. Having been a fundamental part of the 'Quinta del Buitre' Real side (the 'Vulture's Cohort', named after the great Emilio Butragueño: Sanchís, Míchel, Martin Vazquez and Miguel Pardeza, players who were all promoted from the Castilla side – the Real Madrid reserve side – to the first team), a world champion with Maradona and Argentina in 1986, a coach and director at Real, and a central figure in Spanish journalism for years, the quantity (and quality) of Valdano's contacts was enormous. He knew everyone from the king down, he had enjoyed cordial relations with newspaper and television editors, and with the movers and shakers in the capital's media. For a man like Mourinho, who wanted to seal off his working environment while Valdano preached openness, someone like this was a mortal danger. Beyond his history, which spoke for itself, it was known that integrity was a vital part of Jorge's character. In spite of this profoundly decent reputation, José couldn't tolerate the fact that when the team was travelling he would stop to talk to everyone, including the journalists who should be kept away from the hotel and who instead the general director, playing the perfect host, allowed inside. To his mind, maintaining good relations with the media formed a central part of power management, and availability couldn't be kept separate from that: if you support me I'll be available, otherwise I'll triple lock everything. Valdano, on the other hand, had a high view of the subject, and believed that a prestigious institution like Real Madrid should be open regardless as a matter of principle. These two opposing views were irreconcilable. It's said that at that time Mourinho, obsessed with privacy and therefore furious when stories from the dressing room filtered into the media, was convinced that it was Valdano himself who was the mole who was spreading his secrets, and as a result did everything he could to marginalise him. I've never believed that, José is too intelligent to misunderstand Valdano's integrity: the reason for the war, clearly linked to the past, was in their different methods of management. It was no coincidence that Florentino Pérez, when he announced Valdano had been sacked on 25 May, would talk about the 'need to restructure the organisation of the club in order to modernise it'.

Although the final curtain wouldn't come down on him for another month, Mourinho's decisive move to push the general director over the edge came in the hours after his triumph in Valencia. Real Madrid celebrated the Copa del Rey triumph, their least important objective, with a victory parade.

After returning to Madrid after the game, the players found an open-top bus waiting for them at Barajas airport to take them to the Plaza de Cibeles, where thousands of fans were waiting for them – in the middle of the night – around its famous fountain.

There was a bizarre incident when Sergio Ramos dropped the cup under the wheels of the coach, and thankfully the driver noticed in time before it was crushed completely. But the scene was full of Blanco joy and pride, which was pointedly passionate to show just how important a victory against Barcelona had become for the fans. Guardiola and Messi's team had been an ongoing nightmare for years, one which threatened to continue for a long time: with the victory in Valencia, together with the his success in the previous year's Champions League semi-final that prevented the Catalans from parading the European trophy at the Bernabéu, Mourinho had confirmed that he was the only working kryptonite against Barça's superpowers. At that point, he could demand anything. On the Paseo de la Castellana, he was a god. José didn't have to ask twice: he called for Jorge Valdano's head and he got it, even if his official departure was delayed until the end of the season.

Less than a year after his arrival, the biggest and most famous club in the world was in the palm of his hand.

●

BACK IN THE DRESSING ROOM AFTER THE PRESS conference, Pep Guardiola found Leo Messi still in tears and his Spanish internationals furious with the behaviour of their Madrid compatriots. Villa, in particular, suspected that their opponents had been given new instructions, of beating the Catalan players first and then accusing them of simulation. That was what Arbeloa, for example, had done to him. In reality Barcelona should have predicted this strategy, because Sergio Busquets' well-established tendency for simulation – exposed as a cheat by a TV camera the previous year when he got Inter's Thiago Motta sent off – was too good an opportunity not to be exploited in the battle of images. But they didn't. Guardiola spends every post-match fairly distant from his players, and this time was no exception: primarily because he wanted to isolate himself to calmly analyse what had happened, but also because he prefers not to disturb the dressing room dynamic, especially after a disappointing result. However, he confided to Estiarte that the climate created around the four *Clásico* deeply bothered him, because he was forced into indescribable exertion in order to manage the 'war' off the pitch. Guardiola was in a cold fury, tinged with regret at how he had dealt with such a major challenge, against an opponent of the quality and tradition of Real Madrid, and what he should do instead now that Mourinho had conclusively dragged him into a highly personal one-on-one. Pep would rather spend his days studying tactical solutions to play to Leo Messi's strengths and limit Cristiano Ronaldo, but instead he was forced to continually go over Barcelona's values and his way of understanding the game so that he wouldn't be caught unprepared for the dialectical challenge that Mourinho turned the dial up in with every passing day. On the flight back to Barcelona from Valencia, Guardiola said to his friend that 'you have no idea how hard it is to endure all this' before trying to catch some sleep.

●

THERE WAS NO TRAINING THE NEXT DAY, BUT even so Pep was still sat in front of the video player in his office, working out how he had been cornered by Mourinho in the first half at the Mestalla. While the confusion of very tight deadlines meant that he was initially underappreciated by the press, the result of playing extra time after a 9.30 kick-off time, it was Mesut Ozil who was identified as the key man, who had played in a false 9 position in a front line also containing Ronaldo and Di Maria. Incidentally, with regard to what was said above, there were three centre-forwards on the bench: Higuaín and Benzema were left unused, only Adebayor was brought on midway through the second half when Özil had nothing left to give. Guardiola studied and restudied the German's movements, but after a while he was forced to say enough is enough, because he had promised his wife, Cristina, a sophisticated evening for days. In reality, 'sophistication' is a big word for Pep, because when he goes out it is usually to Manel concerts, the Catalan pop band that he likes so much. That evening they were playing at the Teatro Romea, and Pep and Cristina went there like any other couple, and had the presence of mind to go into the stalls as the lights went down in order to avoid attracting attention. But it was a pointless exercise: just as the two were slipping stealthily towards their seats the lights went back on, the audience jumped to their feet and burst into thunderous applause, which was joined by the band themselves up on the stage.

It was an intensely emotionally charged moment, which Guardiola remembers clearly even now: Barcelona had, ultimately, just lost a final against Real Madrid, and in football gratitude and recognition are extremely transient concepts. Those people, however, wanted to reiterate their absolute support in him, which was heartfelt and full of intelligent wisdom. Two years before, as we've seen, at another Manel gig the spectators lovingly implored him to sign a new contract, but after being set off on the most incredible run of success in the club's history, it was easy, almost obligatory in a way, to publicly support him. After his Barcelona had lost for a second time against the awful Mourinho – first Inter, now Real – this support had an altogether different meaning: we're with you Pep, lead us into battle because with you leading us we're sure we – and our values – will prevail. How well the famous Manel played that night isn't known, but what is certain is that Guardiola came out of the theatre, holding Cristina's hand, looking a rejuvenated man. In the absence of the club taking a strong position, and as we've seen it's clear there were some communication problems, it was the unconditional support of the fans that revitalised him.

SIX

FRIDAY 22 APRIL WAS THE DAY BEFORE THE LEAGUE
resumed, with six games remaining for both sides. Given that the
two teams would meet again in the first leg of the Champions
League semi-final the following Wednesday, their respective
matches were brought forward to Saturday: Real were returning
to the Mestalla for a delicate match against third-placed Valencia at 6pm, while Barcelona hosted the dangerous Osasuna at
8pm. The title wouldn't be decided whatever happened – the
Catalans had an eight-point advantage – but either way it was
Mourinho who had the more difficult task. Both coaches had a
number of changes in mind, after the first two games had virtually decided the league and definitively decided the cup, so it was
clear to everyone that the 'series' would be won by whoever went

through in the Champions League. To everyone, that is, except Mourinho and Guardiola; the two continued to deny that the four games in 18 days were interconnected, and clearly from a practical perspective they were right. Since the four games were being played in three different tournaments, it was unnecessary to point out their independence from each other. However, what the two continually failed to recognise in their various press conferences was the psychological impact that each Clásico had on the next one, and therefore how the four games taken together would inevitably result in a winner and a loser. Mourinho took this attitude for tactical reasons, and in fact he was the first to launch a frontal attack after seeing a chink in his rival's armour. Guardiola, on the other hand, truly believed it: he didn't want the conflict, he didn't feel at ease, and he repeated the mantra of not getting emotionally involved to himself. But as we saw at the end of the cup final, this effort was costing him a huge amount of nervous energy, and it was starting to run out. When he met the press that Friday, the day before the game with Osasuna at the Camp Nou, he couldn't resist being sarcastic when one young journalist asked him if he would consider it to be a failure if he finished the season with only the league title in the trophy cabinet: 'Yes, it would be a disaster', Pep replied, with the look of a man running out of patience, 'it would be the end of the cycle. If we only win La Liga, we should change the president, the coach and most of the players.'

There is a correct way to phrase every question, and hopefully that young man learned from the lesson the coach taught him. He then became more serious, and acknowledged the urgency of putting the league to bed: 'I'm probably a good coach, but I'm not so good that I can win every competition I take part in. No one is. That said, the league isn't over and you can imagine how much we want to finish it off as soon as possible. This tournament is the one that really shows how good each team is.' If, according to Mourinho's definition, the Champions League is a tournament won in the detail, there's no doubt that it's the league that best reflects the quality of a coach's work, for the sole reason that it runs from August to May. The live-or-die direct clashes bring other qualities to the fore: holding your nerve, courage, speed of thought, reactivity. After the previous November's 5-0 defeat at the Camp Nou, Mourinho understood that he needed more than a year to go toe to toe against Barcelona over a season, but that the chances in a head-to-head like the Copa del Rey final or a two-legged European tie – more similar to an ordeal – might offer him better chances of success. Forced into a situation that he wasn't entirely comfortable with, Guardiola had to admit he had a problem with his squad: Éric Abidal was recovering after his first liver operation, Adriano had got injured at the Mestalla and his season was finished, Puyol was training separately in the hope that he would be ready for Wednesday, and Maxwell was in pain and didn't know when he would be fit again. Who would play left back? 'Next season we'll have to evaluate the price of competing to win every competition.' In other words, Barcelona would need to make extra signings, revising – with Guardiola's consent – one of the rules he had imposed: a small squad to avoid too many unhappy players on the bench or sitting up in the stands, and if the need arose there would always be a youth team player he could rely on.

Burned by the failure of the Ibrahimović deal, who was sent

back to Italy at a loss of €40 million, the coach returned to the model of his mentor, Johan Cruyff: all of Barcelona's teams should play in the same way, from the kids to the first team, in order to make it easier for players to transition from one team to the next. Those who go up through the teams know their tactical jobs perfectly; they only need to increase the speed and intensity of its application. 'Ours is a complex game,' Pep always said, 'Before a new player comes in I tell them it will take time and hard work to learn, but a player promoted from the *cantera* already knows how to do it. So the players we buy have to take the weeks spent learning how to play our style of football into account. In other words, they have to be top players.' Naturally, that's not to say Ibra isn't. In his case the problem was jealousy, both Zlatan of Messi and Messi of Zlatan. As soon as he was elected, Rosell found himself having to resolve the problem: Milan played the deal to perfection, holding their offer back until the last moments of the transfer window when Barça, pressed internally by Guardiola who didn't want to even cast eyes on the Swede any more, were forced to accept just over €20 million a year after paying €40 million plus Eto'o. Financially, it was a disaster. It's also worth noting that in the previous year's Champions League semi-final, Mourinho himself had taken it upon himself to whisper in Pep's ear that the game wasn't over, despite Thiago Motta's dismissal. It was an unusual incident, made even stranger by the fact that the Catalan coach was talking to Ibra on the touchline. Mind games or not, the relationship between Mou and the Swedish forward had always been excellent, leading to them reuniting at Manchester United; on the other hand, Pep's relationship with Ibrahimović was effectively over after that semi-final.

●

IT'S NOW EASTER SATURDAY. THE BREAKING SPRING

saw people flock to the beach at Malvarrosa, and the restaurants lining the streets of the wonderful city of Valencia were filled by Real Madrid fans who had stayed there since the Copa del Rey final the previous Wednesday. The Las Arenas hotel, in particular, seemed like the Bernabéu grandstand's holiday resort. Compared to the previous week, when the people of Madrid waited for the visit of Barcelona with baited breath after Guardiola's five successive wins – the last of which was the *manita* – the atmosphere had completely changed. Over the course of two games, Mourinho had given back dignity and courage to the point of arrogance to previously frustrated supporters. No one seemed to doubt the outcome of the Champions League semi-final, the momentum was entirely with Real and their line-up for the game at the Mestalla, which had been announced in the hotel that morning, was testament to the depth of their squad: only two players from the cup-winning side, Casillas and Carvalho (who was suspended for the first leg in the Champions League), started the match, and yet most teams in the world would be envious of the 'alternative' attacking trio of Higuaín, Benzema and Kaká. By this point Pipita had recovered from a serious injury and needed minutes after being on the bench in the previous two Clásicos, Benzema was back on the pitch after sitting on the sidelines in the Copa del Rey final, and Kaká... well, Kaká deserves a separate discussion, because after the injury problems that ruled him out of much of his first two seasons in Madrid, this was his moment to force a return to the starting line-up and not let go of his place.

The game couldn't have gone more smoothly for Real, who benefited from that very Spanish tendency for weaker teams to not even dream of studying a tactical plan to contain a stronger opponent. Valencia's coach was Unai Emery, famous now for the trophies he won with Sevilla and hired in 2016 by the highly ambitious Paris Saint-Germain, but in 2011 he was young and still learning, proved by the fact that he conceded six almost identical goals at home to Real. His defensive line, pushed up towards the midfield, was regularly breached in open play by a simple triangular pass that set up Higuaín three times – and as we've learned by watching him every week at Napoli and Juventus, he doesn't miss those sort of chances – Kaká twice and Benzema once. La Liga is crawling with similar coaches who don't change their tactics at all, even after they've conceded six identical goals (Barça and Real don't usually stop themselves, which is part of the reason for the colossal amount of goals scored at the end of each season by the likes of Messi and Ronaldo), strong in the knowledge that the next day the major newspapers will compliment them on the courage and cohesion they showed, rather than grabbing them by the ear for their laziness to not even think about a way of limiting the damage, which is what happens in Italy. Despite Valencia's acquiescence, however, Real played with the freedom of a team under no pressure, and so Guardiola – who watched the first half at the Mestalla in his office in the Camp Nou before going down to the dressing room – spoke plainly to his team: 'Listen, from now on Real will win all of their games. So we have to do the same, starting tonight.' The Barcelona side that faced Osasuna was also very different to Wednesday's, and in the first half it showed, given that, with the result hanging in the balance at 1-0 in the second half after David Villa's opener, Pep put Iniesta, Xavi and Messi on, and the latter scored the final goal two minutes from the end to make the game safe. José Luis Mendilibar, the Pamplona side's coach, did well to keep the match alive up until the final stages: considering that three years earlier he had lost 8-0 at the Bernabéu with Valladolid, in a manner as bad as it sounds, he had unquestionably taken a step forward. It was no coincidence that Guardiola, who studies his colleagues for a long time, had been feeling slightly anxious about the game ever since Wednesday night.

Three points apiece meant that the gap remained the same, but the fact that there were now only five games left was grist to the mill for Barcelona, who needed it after the Copa del Rey disappointment. But then, in his post-game interview, Guardiola made a startling mistake. While Mourinho ignored any questions about Barcelona, and actually made a point of asking me about Inter's result in the press conference to show my Spanish colleagues how the Champions League wasn't on his mind, Pep took the subject on and slipped up twice. The first slip was saying that if the rumours that UEFA were to put the Portuguese referee Pedro Proença in charge of the first leg turned out to be true, Mourinho would be very happy to have a fellow Portuguese on the pitch, just as he had been pleased with Olegário Benquerença's performance during the Inter-Barcelona tie the previous year (the subtext was that Diego Milito's goal to make it 3-1 in the first leg might have been offside). His second slip was, incredibly, even more naive: going back to the Copa del Rey final, Guardiola brought up Pedro's goal that was ruled out for an offside call 'of just two centimetres, from a linesman with a very good view of it' to underline that it was Barça who, in a very evenly balanced game, had been the team who had gone closest to scoring in normal time. The two statements were cracks that were starting to open up in the defensive dam that Pep had built before the quadruple header, and the Madrid papers gleefully made them into gaping chasms by featuring them on the front pages in their Sunday and Monday editions. It isn't in Guardiola's nature to cause controversy, so in the rare instances when he chooses to attack someone out of the blue it comes across all the more clumsy, even ridiculous. Let's consider his comments on Proença, a top class referee, who took charge of the final at the Euros the following year and would rival Nicola Rizzoli to referee the 2014 World Cup final. UEFA hadn't even shortlisted him for the semi-final first legs, instead earmarking Wolfgang Stark (later selected for the game at the Bernabéu), Velasco Carballo, Damir Skomina, Viktor Kassai and Felix Brych. Some free spirits – to use a euphemism – made up a rumour suggesting Pierluigi Collina wanted to put him in charge, and Guardiola believed it without even checking with his club's officials, giving a needlessly stinging response. It was an unthinkable mistake to make at such a high level. Alerted to his rival's comments upon landing in Madrid, Mourinho didn't sleep until the press office had got him a link to the Camp Nou press conference in full. It doesn't take a great stretch of the imagination to imagine the trace of a smile on his face once he had switched off his computer. It was his turn to speak next, as he had the first press conference before the Champions League tie, scheduled for Tuesday lunchtime. José had 36 hours to prepare his counter-attack.

Before fully dedicating himself to Guardiola, however,

Mourinho masterfully defused the Kaká time-bomb that was about to go off at his feet following the Brazilian's sumptuous performance against Valencia. Even though the Copa del Rey had cheered the atmosphere, bringing the fans over to his side and isolating those sections of the media who were still hostile towards him, there remained an underlying feeling at the Bernabéu that the team was not brimming with technical ability – particularly considering the mountain of talent that was being left on the bench. Wednesday's triumph had also come at the cost of Khedira, who was out for what remained of the season. While he provides great tactical balance, the German is a player little loved by fans and pundits, who complained among themselves that he was taking up a playmaker's position. Deep down Mourinho had already decided to replace him with Lassana Diarra, an even more defensive midfielder, but the pro-Kaká lobby was gaining support, including at boardroom level seeing as the €67 million they had spent on him in the summer of 2009 had hitherto largely proved to be a waste of money. He hadn't played a single minute in the first two games in the series, yet the Valencia game showed that he was in excellent physical condition. What to do?

At the same time as Kaká was helping defeat the league's third-placed team, his wife Carolina Celico was loudly crying out to all her relatives in their beautiful family home in São Paulo, as her waters had broken a few days earlier than expected. Everyone quickly left for the Albert Einstein hospital, but not before leaving a message on Kaká's mobile. He had returned to the dressing room pleased with his best performance since joining Madrid, and left it delighted after hearing the news from Brazil. Mourinho jumped at the chance – one of his best quali-

ties – and as Kaká prepared to ask him for permission, he anticipated the question with a quick nod, saying 'go, go', and Real's
officials booked him a seat on the 11.00 TAM Airlines flight that
night from Madrid to São Paulo. Catching his flight by a hair's
breadth, Kaká couldn't sleep for excitement for the almost the
entire 12-hour flight, and getting off the plane at Guarulhos, the
city's international airport, at 6.00 the following morning, he
found his father Bosco Leite waiting with his newborn. Isabella
had been born during the night, weighing 3kg and 170 grams,
and both she and her mother were in good health. Kaká didn't
even go home. He spent the entire Easter Sunday in the hospital
with Carolina, his first child Luca, who was 3 years old, and little
Isabella. In the evening he went back to the airport to fly back,
relaxed, to Madrid the same night for training the following
afternoon. He arrived there with eyes shining with happiness.
And with tiredness.

We will never know how sincere or how strategic Mourinho's
decision was, but we can consider its effects. Firstly, it showed his
human side, an aspect of his character that is rarely appreciated.
Kaká now had a debt of gratitude to him, and it was more than
opportune that a great player, who was being left on the bench,
was now indebted to him. At a bare minimum, it would delay
his understandable, but inevitably controversial, request to play
more. Secondly, a 24-hour round trip would clearly undermine
the demands to restore Kaká to the team, which was primarily
coming from a large section of the public (60%, according to
one poll) who were clamouring for the last Ballon d'Or winner
not called Messi or Ronaldo to return to action. In this condition, it would be insensitive to ask him to play for more than a

short length of time, and as José's post-match comments would show, that was exactly what he was thinking.

SEVEN

WE LEFT GUARDIOLA IN THE CAMP NOU PRESS
room in a bad mood after his team struggled to victory against
Osasuna, and he was so distracted that he let slip a couple of
ill-judged comments about the upcoming third Clásico. The fact
that it was the Copa del Rey defeat that had left its mark on him,
rather than just him having an off day, was shown by his general
demeanour in front of the microphones. Pep lamented the fact
that Barça were going into the decisive stage of the season with
a limited number of players, and in doing so, despite his fierce
claims to the contrary, he gave credence to those people – and
in his opinion they were many, the majority of observers – who
saw Real as clear favourites to reach the Champions League final
after the game in Valencia. Guardiola isn't the type of person to

be cautious, neither out of superstition nor to deliberately make the opposition the favourites, so his comments could either have been sarcastic, as he had been on the Friday, or simply sincere. By this point Manel Estiarte was very concerned, as his friend's latest increase in his working hours – he was now spending more than 10 hours a day watching videos, leaving his assistant, Tito Vilanova, to take charge of the majority of the training exercises – seemed like folly. He could only voice his thoughts at lunch-time, when he would take him out of the brand new training facility at Sant Joan Despí to go and eat by the sea to try and take his mind off things. But it would be 20 minutes, half an hour at most, before Pep would lower his eyes, and even if he would nod to the question 'Are you listening to me?', Estiarte knew that he wasn't, that his mind was in a rectangular world of 105 metres by 68 metres, a psychological arena in which he was fighting the hardest battle of his life. If the full-back pushes up, the opposing full-back is pushed back. If the centre forward drops off, the attacking midfielder fills the space...Manel could almost hear the sound of his mental gears grinding.

●

GUARDIOLA HAD A PROBLEM WITH HIS TEAM selection and another, more general issue.

The problem with his team regarded his left back, because after Saturday's game Maxwell had been forced into the treat-ment room with a sports hernia, ruling out his third choice after Abidal and Adriano. At this point the only chance he had was in hoping that Puyol recovered by Wednesday, but he had only played for an hour in the last three months, the week before at the Bernabéu. The old captain's knees were in pitiful condition, and by now the plan to convert Mascherano to a centre back to replace him was underway. But Puyol, as poor a state as he was in, continued to personify the passion and competitiveness of Barcelona better than anyone else; Guardiola knew that he would be able to rely on him until the bitter end.

The other problem was more subtle, and it had returned to the fore after David Villa's fine performance against Osasuna, when he had scored for the first time in 11 games. Was it possible that Leo Messi was destroying every strike partner he played with, and after practically forcing the club to get rid of Ibrahimović (that's right: Get. Rid. Of. Ibrahimović), had he thrown a hitherto unstoppable striker like Villa into crisis? On Saturday evening, Leo took a place on the bench with reluctance – as on every rare occasion he is forced to do so – until he came on in the last half hour and scored the second goal. But in the hour that he was off the pitch, Villa played very well. And this coincidence, even though it obviously isn't a coincidence, anguished Guardiola, torn between acting in the interests of the team, which nearly always coincided with those of Messi, and his desire to give all of his players their time in the limelight. In the end he always chooses the first option, but that doesn't mean that he doesn't feel bad for those who are left out. Unlike Zlatan, who was viewed as an outsider by many of those in the dressing room the previous year, Villa was much more integrated with his team-mates, as is only natural for someone who has won the European Championships and the World Cup with Puyol, Xavi and Iniesta, so the problem was a far cry from the tensions of the previous season. But it still existed.

In reality the entire Catalan internal environment's dependence on Messi had already passed the point of no return, even if Leo was yet to turn 24. Except for those devoted followers of the cult of Cristiano Ronaldo, no one denied that he was the best player in the world any longer. Instead, it was his place in history that was being discussed, which was a premature discussion given his age. Asked for his opinion on the great Messi-Maradona debate, Santiago Segurola – a top Spanish journalist – summed up the discussion perfectly when he said that 'Messi is the eternal Maradona'. There is almost never a game when La Pulga doesn't score a fantastic goal, or at least doesn't inspire Barcelona's wonderful style, while Diego occasionally allowed himself to coast through games from time to time, partly because, unlike Leo, he certainly didn't lead an athlete's lifestyle. It was a risky situation to be dependent on such a talented young man, but a young man nonetheless, because his occasional tantrums had to be tactfully dealt with. The previous season, Guardiola was sat on the front row of the team bus coming back from an away game, won with a goal from Ibrahimović, when he received a text message from Messi, sat in the back row, that made his heart stop. It essentially said 'I'm upset to find out I'm not your most important player any more.' While he certainly doesn't have the cruelty of *Game of Thrones'* vicious young King Joffrey, Leo was still a character who needed to be handled very carefully to avoid creating any sort of drama, including, crucially, his potential desire to move clubs. Ever since Joan Laporta, the club's directors have viewed this as a nightmare scenario. During the club's history, Barcelona have often bought the best players in the world – think about phenomenons like Maradona and Ronaldo – but then let them slip away, often to Italian clubs when the lure of the lira was at its strongest. In Messi's case, as he grew up at the club and is therefore more closely connected to it, it has practically been club policy to make concessions to him to ensure he never has the desire to go somewhere else. In some ways this policy was necessary: if one of Leo's representatives had contacted Florentino Pérez at that time (or even now), he would certainly have made him an offer to join los Blancos. To repeat the Figo saga – which took Barcelona years to recover from – with one of the best players in history (if not the best) would have made him an idol at the Bernabéu to his supporters. But Leo's entourage have always ignored any overtures from Madrid.

After being given the Barça job in the late spring of 2008, Guardiola won Messi's confidence in just two moves. The first was political, because that summer it was the Olympics in Beijing and Leo had been called up by coach Sergio Batista, even though Barcelona – who had finished third in La Liga in Rijkaard's final season – were due to play Wisla Krakow in the Champions League preliminary round. The Olympics weren't part of the official FIFA calendar and so Barça appealed to the Court of Arbitration for Sport (CAS) in Lausanne to restore Messi to them – similar cases were subsequently made by Werder Bremen for Diego and Schalke for Rafinha. The highly controversial debate went on for several days while the players were already in China to prepare for the tournament, until the CAS ruled in the clubs' favour. They ruled that the clubs' obligations to the international scene didn't extend to Olympic squads, and therefore if they wanted to recall their players they were free to do so. At that time in early August, Barcelona were on tour in New York, and once he had won his contentious legal battle Laporta, who had pushed heavily for Leo's return, gave Guardiola carte blanche to do what he needed to do to bring him back. Pep was able to get in touch with Leo, which wasn't easy due to the time difference, but he could sense the discomfort of a young man in a great deal of difficulty at the other end of the line. Messi had only won an Under 20s title in 2005 with Argentina, and after being virtually invisible during the World Cup in Germany the following year, the Olympic Games were a chance for his country's fans – many of whom considered him to be a foreigner since they had never seen him play at Boca or River – to finally fall in love with him. Messi had left Argentina for ever at 13 years old, and did so directly from Rosario; up until 2005 no one in Buenos Aires knew who he was. Even today – after a hitherto unsuccessful career with *La Selección* – many people question where his national identity truly lies, the classic argument that always comes up when the team isn't winning. The shock of the last defeat in the Copa América Centenario, with the subsequent statement that he never wanted to play for Argentina again, is testament to an emotional situation that is, at times, unsustainable for him.

His voice trembling, Leo implored his new coach – or rather his future coach, given that the two were yet to meet each other on the pitch – to let him stay in China. Pep had already thought about it before dialling the number, because obtaining La Pulga's support was an essential part of his entry strategy, but he was moved to hear him sounding so desperate, and he quickly gave him his blessing. 'It's fine Leo, I will guarantee the club that we will get through the Champions League tie without you. You can stay at the Olympics, but now I suggest you win them.' The mental tension suddenly released, Messi burst into tears of joy. After a few simple administrative hurdles had been cleared – that his insurance would be paid for by the Argentine FA, for example – he was on the pitch against the Côte d'Ivoire in the first game of the tournament, standing triumphantly alongside Juan Román Riquelme, the old cacique of Argentina who had been irritably watching the young star's rise for some time, convinced that he lacked character. However, Guardiola's concession showed that La Pulga was able to impose himself, and Leo soon felt a special connection in his relationship with his new coach.

Ronaldinho was also at those Olympics, having been sold by Barcelona two weeks before to Milan. It wasn't a great deal for the Italian club: a few good performances aside, for instance when he scored the winning goal in the derby (against Mourinho's Inter), in his two seasons in Serie A the Brazilian prematurely showed that he was finished, his private life so unruly that it cost him his competitive edge at the age of just 28. A few months before I witnessed a very sweet yet melancholic scene in the bowls of the Camp Nou: while I was waiting to interview Andrés Iniesta in the club's offices, I was sat in a position where I could see the short pathway linking the door leading out of the changing room and the players' car park (and since I was sat behind the door, unless the player turned around as soon as they came out then they wouldn't have seen me). Ronaldinho was one of the first to leave, by himself, with a black toiletry bag in his hand, while halfway down the pathway one of the cleaning ladies had started her work with a mop and bucket. It was nice, and unusual, to see the player stop to talk to the woman, a weary middle-aged black lady, a citizen of that world that players generally never even see, let alone visit. Instead Dinho spoke to her for a few minutes, perhaps because he knew her. They were speaking Portuguese rather than Spanish. He may (I was a bit too far away) have asked her something about her daughter, certainly about one of her relatives who was studying, before she, picking up a cloth and wiping the sweat from her forehead, asked him how he was feeling. Ronaldinho made a sad gesture, touching his face as if to say 'I don't recognise myself any more', and the two stood in silence for a long moment. Then Ronaldinho said goodbye, and as they went their separate ways both of them seemed mentally fatigued, perhaps they had recognised that in each other. The Brazilian champion's rapid and continuing decline, akin to Buffalo Bill at the circus, is one of football's small tragedies.

As has been mentioned, it was Guardiola himself who, upon taking charge of Barça, insisted that he was sold. Beyond the fact that his influence on Messi, who naturally idolised him, threatened to take Leo down the ugly route of nights out on the town, Pep's theory was that when the young talent was ready, he mustn't find his path blocked by an aging great, who still normally started even though his ability was the inferior of the two. The old superstar was sold to facilitate the assertion and the handover of responsibility to the young superstar.

'As long as Ronaldinho is here, every important pass will go to him, because that's what everyone is used to doing,' Guardiola explained to Laporta, 'but starting this year I want every crucial pass to go to Messi.'

He made a similar argument about Deco, who was preventing Iniesta from definitively asserting himself, and about Eto'o, who Laporta very wisely defended: in Pep's first year the Cameroonian forward's talent and ruthlessness – 'you don't play finals, you win them' – were vital.

Going back to Ronaldinho, something else was touching about his meeting with Messi at the old Beijing Workers' Stadium for the Olympic semi-final, because the almost straightforward 3-0 victory inflicted by Argentina against Brazil mirrored the changing of the guard at the Blaugrana, which was encapsulated at the end of the game when the pair's embrace felt like they were saying goodbye. Following that semi-final, the prelude to Argentina's victory against Nigeria in the final at the Bird's Nest, I remember the chaotic post-match scenes in the mixed zone; Messi had his usual blank look on his face as he walked past the forest of Argentine microphones, imploring him for an interview, when he stopped just before getting on the bus because someone who worked on a Barcelona radio station had called out to him in Catalan – 'sisplau!' – and he had felt compelled to respond to her. What was that about La Pulga's real nationality...

In any case, the victory in Beijing softened the Argentines' slightly detached attitude towards Messi. Even though in his heart the victory was for the many relatives that he had in Rosario, Leo was very grateful to Guardiola, who – and we're now at his second move, the tactical one – called him into his office when he returned from China to explain the new role he had in mind for him, which can be summed up in one, simple phrase: 'If you do what I tell you, you'll score a hat-trick every game.' Pep's comment was probably just hyperbole, but Messi's performances since then have brought him very close to making it reality. Guardiola created space around Leo to create an attacking system that stylistically isn't too different to what is called 'isolation' in basketball, which had never been implemented in such a specific way in football: in order to create the space for the Argentine to go on one of his devastating runs, where he could quickly dribble past numerous players, his team-mates would position themselves further apart to drag the opposition out of position. Using this method, he would score a staggering number of goals season after season, only followed by – or occasionally in pursuit of – Cristiano Ronaldo: there is no better example of an individual duel in sport than theirs. There's even a date to mark the start of the contest, 2 May, 2009: in the second Clásico of Pep's first season – the 6-2 rout at the Bernabéu – he moved Messi from the right-wing to the centre for the first time, in the role that would become known as the 'false 9'. It wasn't an entirely unprecedented concept, but employing it with a player of Messi's quality would become one of the keys to the Catalans' success in subsequent years. The only downside was the fact that Leo consumed the entire frontline as a result: Eto'o was sold at the end of Guardiola's first season, Ibrahimović was a resounding failure (although the fault for that wasn't entirely his), the great Thierry Henry was in the final stages of a career that had already taken a lot out him by the time he went to Catalonia, and finally there was Pedro. The boy from the Canary Islands had come through the Blaugrana *cantera* as well, and having seen the Messi legend from up close he was willing to make any tactical sacrifice in order to play alongside him (it was no coincidence that he would last the longest, up until Neymar and Luis Suárez redefined the concept of playing alongside Messi). David Villa, who joined amid great enthusiasm, which was partly down to his congenial personality, would score a number of important goals, including a brace in the *manita* Clásico, but in the end not even he would be a complete success, and, again, the fault for that was not entirely his.

EIGHT

THE FIRST SIGN A STORM WAS BREWING CAME
on Monday, when Sergio Ramos said in an interview that he
was amazed by Guardiola's recent comments. 'Incredible, now
they're criticising referees who get decisions right. I've had
enough of this.' Barcelona took this signal very seriously, and
an order to remain calm was immediately issued at Sant Joan
Despí. In the meantime, the Madrid radio stations – who will
play a vital role in increasing the tensions in this story – banged
on about it incessantly, and there was no taxi in either city that
wasn't tuned into a station talking about football. Complaining
about each other took precedence over sensible and, above all,
impartial analysis. In both cities. A little tongue in cheek, I called
them the Radio Thousand Hills, named after the Rwandan ra-

dio station that propagated the genocide of the Tutsis by the Hutus. Fortunately, this situation wasn't bloody, but using the media to incite violence is a tried and tested practice in war-torn countries. And ultimately we're talking about a war, obviously a cold war, because Catalonia's desire for independence is well known and other regions, such as the Basque country, are closely watching how the situation develops. The adjective Real (royal) deeply hurts every Barça supporter no matter who it relates to: there isn't just Real Madrid, but Real Sociedad, Real Betis, Real Zaragoza. The monarchy is an ever-present symbol of Spanish unity, and is therefore hated by every separatist.

In the dressing room, Mourinho was sending out mixed messages. First he reminded the team that they should go in hard on Barcelona, because the time they had committed the fewest number of fouls (16) was also the time they were humiliated 5-0 in the first La Liga meeting, whereas the 27 fouls in the Mestalla (including extra time) had led them to lift the Copa del Rey. That said, he also told his players not to overdo it and to be careful, because in Europe people had a lot of respect for Barcelona and referees would adapt accordingly, unlike Undiano Mallenco the week before, who had let some things slide. At the same time, the Madrid media harshly criticised the assigned referee, the German Wolfgang Stark, whose appointment not only brought back memories of a penalty he had recently denied Real in the Round of 16 at Lyon (for a handball by Yoann Gourcuff), but most of all an incident that occurred at the World Cup the year before. It so happened that Stark, before Argentina-Nigeria, had said that he was a fan of Leo Messi ('watching him play is a real pleasure' were his exact words) and, at the end of the game, he had asked for his shirt as a memento. All hell broke loose! The most moderate interpretation of this was that the Champions League tie between Real and Barça would be refereed by a Messi ultra. Once again, the Spanish media's fixation of searching through referees' personal histories before a big match had paid off. The spark that would ignite the high levels of tension was about to lit.

•

ON TUESDAY MORNING, THE DAY BEFORE THE game, the press room at Valdebebas – Real Madrid's vast training complex adjacent to the city's Barajas airport – looked like the General Assembly of the United Nations. Hundreds of journalists were crowded in like commuters on a Japanese metro, the last seat was taken an hour before the start, soon there was hardly anywhere left to stand, and the heat from the lights of the cameras made a pleasant late April morning feel like a scorching summer's day. The air was thick with the sense a storm was coming, and indeed we were all there to witness the incident, including Americans, Brazilians and Argentines who had just landed and raced across the short distance from the airport by taxi. Naturally Mourinho had organised the conference for the perfect time because all the flights, including intercontinental flights, had landed comfortably. He is a consummate professional, even down to the last detail.

While the clubs were enjoying such great success, many of the world's best players were playing for either Barça or Real at the time, the press rooms in Madrid and Barcelona had transformed into something like the cantina bar in *Star Wars*, the unforgettable melting pot of citizens from across the galaxy created by

George Lucas' imagination. In the same way, in Spain there were obviously a lot of Spaniards, but also many Catalans, who insist on speaking their language – it isn't a dialect, they swear, but an authentic language – including, and most of all, on official occasions. Which is sometimes a hindrance. For example: Puyol, to name one champion of Barça and of Catalanism, speaks in his language rather than in Castilian, and UEFA have done nothing to stop him. When the Blaugrana face a German team, I can't understand anything – I don't speak German – and not even the translator can help me, because he translates into Catalan. It wouldn't be a problem if he spoke in Spanish, but obviously that carries a symbolic political value with it that Barça – 'the unarmed army of Catalonia', remember Montalbán? – cannot afford to bear. If these are the two tribes who dominate this 'cantina bar', in third place numerically are the English: many of them arrived in Spain in Beckham's wake, the most 'marketable' player in history, although it's true that many freelancers have lived there for years. When David had had enough, leaving Madrid for Los Angeles, none of them returned to London, because life in Spain is too good: they simply moved to Barcelona, on the coast (speaking of the good life), to cover Ronaldinho and the rising star Messi, who, in their own turn, also drew throngs of Brazilians and Argentines. These are people who are used to watching their country's best players from a distance, but the pleasures of Barcelona convinced them to move a bit closer. Much closer, in fact. A few Italians report from Madrid and Catalonia as well, then there are French reporters who also deal with Africa, the Portuguese who also specialise in the Brazilian transfer market, various South Americans, a few Mexicans, two

Germans, a Turk and increasingly numerous Asians – although you never know the size of their audiences, it's better to err on the side of caution and consider them to be large. At the time the major newspapers' correspondents caroused in well-known restaurants – not for much longer though, soon the crisis would hit them too – while the freelancers scraping by made do with beer and tapas, but it was a dream to be in that environment: people from across the world were all excitedly talking about football and enjoying themselves ahead of games of a level rarely seen before. The Clásico is a spiritual place.

Mourinho entered the press room from the side door next to the stage. He was in a suit but, unlike other times, he was freshly shaven. In his own way, on the global stage, he was dressed to kill. He gave a friendly, somewhat theatrical greeting to one of the Italian journalists who had arrived for the game, before looking down at the number of TV cameras set out on a platform at the back of the room, and while he was hiding his emotions his face was very attentive. José was reminiscent of a tennis player at the start of the fourth set, two sets to one ahead and preparing to serve: he hasn't won yet, but he feels confident and is lining up an ace to start the next, perhaps decisive, game. He has had three days to think about a verbal stratagem that would knock Guardiola sideways after his negative comments on Saturday. There was no doubt he was about to drop a bombshell; the only question was how powerful it would be. The tension was at its peak. It wasn't even remotely conceivable that the first question would be about anything other than the referee, and in fact it began with the revelation of how nervous Barcelona were that Proenca might be assigned to the game. Mourinho immediately made it clear that, today, he wouldn't be holding back.

'I think there is something more important than the referee, and more important even than the pressure they have exerted to ensure Proença doesn't referee'. Javi Tamames, the press officer who attends all the press conferences, ran a hand across his face, as if he had foreseen something. Mourinho never tells him what he will say in advance, partly because it isn't in his nature, and partly because once a week Javi plays football with a team of foreign journalists stationed in Madrid. He has never revealed anything confidential, he is a very serious professional, but in these testing circumstances the coach's inner circle suspected him of colluding with the enemy, and in fact Javi wouldn't last much longer. 'The main thing is that we are starting a new cycle with this match, we are entering a new chapter in history.' Mourinho spoke in total silence, which is incredible in a room crowded with more journalists than it was clearly capable of holding. He pulled a bit on his shirt sleeves, as if to keep his hands free. 'Up until now there were two groups of coaches. One very, very small group of coaches who don't talk about referees. There are very few of them, very few...' Mourinho shakes his head as he says this, oscillating between respect for such morally superior colleagues and incredulity, 'and a second very big group, in which I'm included. This group criticises referees when they make big mistakes. We're human, and I'll say again that I am part of this group, we're unable to control our frustrations when a referee's decision unfairly costs us. But we're also happy to recognise when a referee has done his job well, when he has been successful.' Up until now Mourinho has almost been talking to himself, his head bowed, though not to read, he doesn't have pieces of paper in front of him, he doesn't need them, but instead to find the right words to introduce his argument, making sure that his audience has independently reached the same conclusion he is about to give them. Now Mou raises his head, and it is as though he is looking into the eyes of every journalist in the room. 'After what Pep said the other night, we've started a new era because there is now a third group. It's a group that, at the moment, is made up of only one person, which is him...' The silence is broken by a short laugh, someone has just understood, while Mou puts his hands together and starts moving them up and down, to underline the enormity of what he is saying, 'and it's a group that criticises the referee when they get decisions right. This is completely new to me, something that is completely new to the world of football...' Now more people are sniggering. 'We'll see what happens from now on. He has many supporters, because of the fantastic football that his team plays and because he is a fantastic coach. We'll see if they'll support him while he's part of this group too, who criticise a referee when he makes the correct decision.' The final few words were said almost indignantly.

●

THE SILENCE OF A FEW MOMENTS BEFORE IS JUST a memory. Many people have switched on their phones to pass on what Mourinho has said to their editors, they even have the headline ready and it's very, very juicy. But he hasn't finished. Sat next to him, Marcelo, the player chosen for the press conference, watches him with an expression caught between amusement and bewilderment. Marcelo is a cheerful sort, someone who lives a carefree life, and it's no coincidence that he is Ronaldo's best friend in the dressing room, who has a more dour character. But even Marcelo, light-hearted as he is, has sensed how intense the coach's comments are, and now he was as curious as anyone to see how far he would go. He had already answered his full allocation of questions, but he didn't seem to be in a rush to join his team-mates in the restaurant. He knew that the show he was witnessing just then would be talked about for a long time to come.

'In my opinion, it all started with the scandal at Stamford Bridge. Ever since that evening, Pep hasn't felt comfortable with referees making correct decisions. Last year he played against us when we had 10 men, this year they nearly went out against Arsenal...That's how it is; when the referee makes the right call he doesn't like it.' A little bit of background information is necessary here. The 'scandal at Stamford Bridge' was the second leg of the Champions League semi-final in 2009, decided by an injury time goal from Iniesta after Tom Henning Øvrebø had denied Chelsea two clear penalties; the reference to the game with 10 men was another semi-final, Barcelona-Inter in 2010, during which Thiago Motta was sent off after half an hour for a contentious second yellow card (he did touch Sergio Busquets in the face, but he went down theatrically feigning much more serious contact) by Frank De Bleeckere; finally Arsenal, in this season's Round of 16 second leg, had Robin Van Persie sent off at the Camp Nou when they were still going through on aggregate for an even more contentious second yellow card (given by Massimo Busacca when he kicked the ball away after being flagged offside). Mourinho's argument was crystal clear and equally cutting: Guardiola is so used to being helped by referees that when they

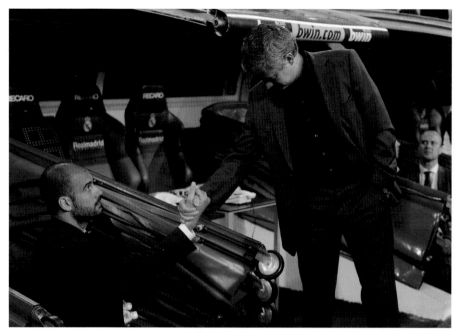

Jose Mourinho and Pep Guardiola shake hands before the first of four Clásico's in eighteen days. Despite the hostilities that would follow, the pair would repeat this ritual in the next two games. (Getty)

Captains Carles Puyol and Iker Casillas, both of whom made their Spain debut in the year 2000, also share a handshake as they walk on to the pitch for the La Liga clash. Things would soon turn sour. (Getty)

Xavi, Pepe, Sergio Busquets and Andrés Iniesta surround referee Muñiz Fernández as tempers begin to flare. (Getty)

Raúl Albiol becomes the first man to see red over the course of the 18 days, after hauling down David Villa in the penalty area. Lionel Messi scored the ensuing penalty. (Getty)

Pepe, never one to shy away from confrontation, tries to get in the head of Messi by suggesting there is something wrong with him. (Getty)

It wasn't just the Madrid players trying to put the Argentine star off his game – the Bernabéu crowd also gave it their best shot. (Getty)

Concentrated on the task at hand, Mourinho looks on from the dugout prior to the Copa del Rey final. (Getty)

His opposite number, meanwhile, looks a little dazed ahead of a tense evening. (Getty)

In amongst all the animosity, a brief moment of harmony as Dani Alves and Cristiano Ronaldo shake hands. (Getty)

Conflict was never far away, though. Here Barcelona winger Pedro wags his finger in the face of Ricardo Carvalho. (Getty)

After a trademark Ronaldo header secures victory for Real in extra time, Marcelo celebrates. (Getty)

One Madrid fan lets his Catalan counterparts know what he thinks of them at the Mestalla. (Getty)

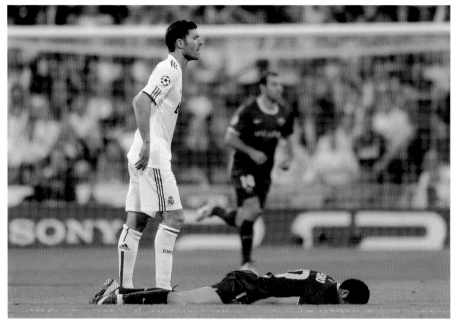

Pedro lying poleaxed on the floor in the first leg of the Champions League semi-final at the Bernabéu. International teammate Xabi Alonso stands over him. (Getty)

Captain Casillas, who would later be dropped by Mourinho after attempting reconciliation with Xavi, holds the cup aloft. (Getty)

Sergio Ramos jabs his finger into Gerard Piqué's chest. Despite success together at international level, the pair remain intense rivals. This mutual clash of personalities began when Pique made a hand gesture to Ramos after the latter was sent off at the Camp Nou during Barcelona's 5-0 win earlier in the campaign. (Getty)

A half-time brawl breaks out between players and staff from both sides. Pinto, Barcelona's substitute keeper on the night, saw red for his involvement. (Getty)

Mourinho – in typical Mourinho fashion – has a quiet word with Barcelona captain Puyol after Pepe's red. (Getty)

Often the chief villain in the series, the Madrid boss receives a sending off of his own, and so takes up his position in the stands, still particularly close to the dugout. (Getty)

Scrapping aside, there was a game of football with an awful lot at stake to be played. Here Messi celebrates after giving Barcelona a crucial lead after wonderful work from substitute Ibrahim Afellay. He would soon make it 2-0 with a quite stunning solo effort. (Getty)

A steward stands in the pouring rain at a deserted Camp Nou before the second leg. Barcelona would go into the game with a 2-0 lead. Mourinho was banned from the ground. (Getty)

A pitch invader throws a traditional Catalan hat ('barretina') at Ronaldo. Marcelo folds his hands in weary antipathy behind. (Getty)

Pedro gives Barcelona the lead on the night ten minutes into the second half, effectively ending the tie as a contest, even though Marcelo would later equalise for the visitors. (Getty)

After three weeks of jibing with Mourinho and putting intense pressure on himself, Guardiola celebrates progression to another final with a relieved roar. (Getty)

A touching moment after a trying few weeks: Éric Abidal is lofted into the air by his teammates at full time. The French international had only just returned following an operation to remove a tumour on his liver. (Getty)

make the right decision, he can't accept it. The icing on the cake was when he wished Stark good luck: 'I honestly hope that he has the quality and the luck – yes, you need that too – to referee this successfully. I don't want a referee who helps my team, but instead at the end of the game both clubs should be satisfied with the job he's done...' A final, slightly longer pause then came his final volley. 'But I know that isn't possible, because if he doesn't make a mistake in his favour then Pep won't be happy.'

We're in thermonuclear war.

The press officer chose the next question from the many raised hands, but the coach wasn't looking at him, he wanted to make sure his direct attack on Guardiola – he had called him Pep for the first time – became fixed in the audience's collective memory. It was a carefully planned move, and he needed to take a moment to gather his thoughts because its effect was explosive. It was the eve of a Champions League semi-final between Real Madrid and Barcelona, perhaps the biggest rivalry in world football, but at this point it was comparable to two other sports: the psychological violence of a great chess match, with its mental games aimed at annihilating the opponent (Mourinho's 'mind games' are an Alex Ferguson copyright), and the physical violence of an all-in-wrestling match, in which there are few rules to see who really is the strongest. José evaluates the reactions in the room with a false casualness; he knows all the most important, most influential journalists are there, and he has spoken directly to them. They have taken the time to come in person, unwilling to leave such an important press conference to field reporters. There, now he beckons to Javi: having imperceptibly relaxed, he's now ready for another question. After making a cutting remark, his communication strategy dictates he follows it up with something like a joke, or at least a smile. The skill lies in adapting his answer – calculated and planned in advance – to whatever question he is asked. The person chosen by Javi wants to know what has changed since the day of the *manita* up to now, obviously from a 5-0 defeat to winning the Copa del Rey and being favourites in the Champions League. Too easy, for Mou.

'I'm exactly the same motivator and the same coach that lost 5-0 against Barcelona. Exactly the same. I don't have magic potions.' Some might read a sarcastic jibe in Mou's words towards the accusations of doping that were being made against Barcelona at the time, which had aroused a justifiably angry reaction: the accusations were generally being propagated by media outlets close to Real, and the team were often subject to random drugs tests. I don't think that was Mourinho's intention: when the Portuguese decides to send a message he makes very deliberate pauses, but here he was speaking very directly as if there was no subliminal message. 'I simply tell my players...', the joke is on its way, 'and these aren't my words, but those of someone called Albert...', a knowing pause, 'Albert Einstein...' José smiles widely, and it's as though he has allowed those present to do the same; what had been a tense atmosphere suddenly became jovial, his control over his audience once again is absolute. It seemed more like a group therapy session than a press conference. 'He once said that the only driving force more powerful than steam, electricity or nuclear power is willpower. And Albert wasn't an idiot...' a final brief pause, so that the idea that Einstein wasn't stupid takes hold quickly, like the famous 'I'm not a fool' of his first day at Inter, 'I tell my players we can do things with willpower.' Like rising from the ashes of disaster to winning a trophy in just a few months.

Mourinho smiled at the hustle and bustle of the press room, where us journalists, overwhelmed with the urge to leave to run back to our hotels and start writing, moved like a crazed Pac-Man. Excitement reigned because after so much tension, Mou's press conference was a declaration of full-scale war, where the Catalan journalists in attendance were the enemy's ambassadors. Some of them weren't calling their newspapers, but their contacts they had inside Barcelona to get a response, an immediate reaction, even an insulting reply – that would suffice as well. Mourinho got up slowly, making his usual little jokes with the Italian reporters about Inter, and left satisfied with the job he had done. Guardiola had wanted to underline how well-balanced the Copa del Rey final was, certainly not to stigmatise the referee and his assistants for a correct decision, but his naivety had given Mourinho the opportunity to fundamentally undermine the myth of the Blaugrana's sportsmanship, that apparent moral superiority that Pep and his ways of understanding the duel are widely accredited with. There was all the deceitfulness of a fallen angel in his discourse; excluded from paradise and twice refused entry, he now believed he had found the key.

José Mourinho can be as cunning as the serpent in the Garden of Eden. The metaphor, used by Primo Levi to describe another prisoner at Auschwitz who was able to survive due his inhuman guile, can also be applied to the Portuguese coach, because his superior intelligence allows him to dominate every aspect of the verbal confrontation. Nothing can stand in his way as he protects his own interests at any cost. In his incredible book *If This Is a*

Man, Levi looked back at Henri – the young man who knew how to survive like no one else – and wrote that he would have liked to know what his life was like outside the camp, but confessed that he didn't want to see him again, obviously upset by the moral price he had paid to survive in an environment where one person's salvation fatally came at the expense of others. In a much less tragic situation, Mourinho used his grey cells to create mental paths that were inscrutable on the whole, at least at the start, in order to take his target almost by surprise. These aren't just the mind games of Ferguson, but a comprehensive strategy on a vast scale that develops before our eyes, one move at a time, but which the supreme chess master from Setubal had seen right from the start.

Mourinho is the most talented puppet master ever seen in the world of football.

●

NATURALLY BARCELONA'S PLAYERS, GATHERED in the Eurostar Tower on the Paseo della Castellana, not far away from the stadium, heard what Mourinho had said in real time, and it quickly became impossible for them to rest during their afternoon break before the final training session. Crowds of people converged in the players' bedrooms, and the anger towards the Portuguese coach was palpable. Piqué and Xavi were the most offended, but the others also felt that they had reached their limit. Guardiola spent a long time lying on his bed looking up at the ceiling, as if he thought he would find something written up there that would tell him the best way to react. It was clear to him that he needed to give a similarly hostile response, which would be a fatal blow to his self-assurance. It didn't really matter. He had known this moment would come ever since Mourinho's first day in charge at Real Madrid. Even Estiarte hardly had an opportunity to advise him this time. Pep preferred to remain alone, aware this was a turning point, and he didn't want to share the responsibility of choosing between war and peace.

It was his duty; it was up to him to make his decision without involving, and therefore putting at risk, other people.

He came down to the lobby 10 minutes early, the coach to take them to the stadium hadn't even arrived. 20 Barça fans cheered him from behind the barriers set up by hotel security, and on another day Pep would respond with at least a nod – he is very good-mannered if introverted – but on that afternoon he didn't even see them. His mind was completely focused on the field of battle, which for once wasn't the football pitch but the press room. He didn't say a word on the coach, escorted by police on its way to the Bernabéu, but listened carefully to every word the players were saying to each other, a low murmur that increased the anger inside him, because Barça were in a difficult situation and needed to focus on their game, but instead Mourinho had succeeded in turning the tables and increasing the match's emotional stakes to new extremes. He also knew that he needed to respond so as not to appear weak in the dressing room. His players knew and respected him, but this was a situation where it was impossible for their blood not to boil.

Guardiola hid his emotions with the utmost care, trying to get his players' minds back to where they should have been, which was on the tactical plans for the next day's game. He was even more demanding than usual during the training session, he shrugged his shoulders when he was told the grass on the pitch was long – he knew that already, and to him a predicted obstacle was no longer an obstacle – and grimaced when news came from the doctor that Iniesta had been ruled out after failing his final fitness test, and would spend the game sat in the stands. After Maxwell dropped out as well, the team was effectively decided, because at that point only the injury-ravaged Puyol could play left back. It really was an ugly business, but Guardiola would worry about it later. Now he needed to respond to Mourinho to ensure that the game's psychological momentum, already with Real, didn't become impossible to overcome. At the end of training the coach had a shower, and when he crossed the dressing room to leave for his press conference he had the look of a soldier about to go into battle.

However, Barça wanted to lower the volume, not raise it still further, which is why Rosell sent Andoni Zubizarreta, Barcelona's Basque ex-goalkeeper who was their sporting director, to the dressing room to make sure that Guardiola didn't lose his head. The two are old friends and team-mates, and in a way it was the coach who solicited his appointment, because when Rosell replaced Laporta the then sporting director, Txiki Beguiristain – now a director of football at Manchester City – handed in his resignation. He, like Guardiola and Zubizarreta, was part of Cruyff's Dream Team, and while the coach was very sorry to see him go, it was logical to replace him with someone who was not only one of the new president's confidants but also who wasn't unpopular with the coach.

'Pep, are you calm? The president doesn't want you to respond to Mourinho. We thought we'd send Mascherano to the press conference with you, he knows how to count to 10 before answering a provocative question. The president wants everything to be about what happens on the pitch. Are we agreed?' Guardiola nodded quickly, he was just in a hurry to get in front of the microphones. Elegant in his grey suit, Chemi Teres, the Barcelona press officer for the international media, guided him towards the Bernabéu press room. Inside, all the journalists who had been to Valdebebas that morning were present as well as many others; some of them weren't even sports journalists, but had simply been attracted by the smell of blood. At that time, there was nothing more captivating in the world than the titanic duel between José Mourinho and Pep Guardiola.

Chemi was nervous, clearly impatient as he watched the usual rigmarole of the photo opportunity – everyone lined up in front of the flashing cameras for a couple of long minutes –with the demeanour of an English lord. He had to bite his tongue, because the photographer closest to the coach, wildly snapping away like there was no tomorrow, was the club's own photographer taking pictures for their website. But before long he called for calm – 'thank you, thank you' – and reminding everyone of the procedures: the first language would be Castilian, then English, and finally there would be room for Catalan. Guardiola wasn't listening to him; his mind was clearly somewhere else, focusing on what he was about to say. Wearing a club tracksuit, the jacket open over his polo shirt due to the heat, he took small sips from his ever-present bottle of water, and every so often would raise a hand to his face to stroke his four-day beard. It's amazing how he has become virtually bald over the course of three seasons, aged by a stress that was hard to imagine at the time, but would become clear a year later when he chose to take a sabbatical year. The signal came when he tilted his head left and right to stretch the muscles in his neck. It was time to begin.

The first question was a given, partly because Chemi was the one to choose who would ask a question. David Bernabeu, from TV channel *Cuatro*, asked him if he had been told about what Mourinho had said: with his own channel's cameras there though, the journalist couldn't simply ask the question but had to provide a brief précis of the content of the Portuguese's press conference. Guardiola nodded a couple of times, impatient. He seemed like a sprinter waiting for the starting gun. The first time was a false start because the microphone wasn't working, and Chemi fixed it by tapping on it cautiously, perhaps fearing an electric shock. The second time, we were underway.

'First of all, good afternoon. *Señor* Mourinho has referred to me explicitly, he called me Pep and so I'll call him José. I don't know which camera is *Señor* José's,' he raised his gaze towards the back of the room, where the TV crews were, then lowered it again as he cracked a little smile, 'I guess they all are. Tomorrow at 8.45 we'll face each other here on the pitch. Off the pitch he has won, he's been winning all season and he'll keep winning. He can have his own personal Champions League for it to take home and enjoy alongside all the others he's won. We'll compete for the other one here, maybe we'll win, maybe we'll lose, in reality he normally wins, that's what history says. We're happy with smaller victories, trying to get the world to admire us and we're very, very proud of that. I could have come here with a list of incidents to compare with the examples he gave, but we'd never finish if I had. He remembered Stamford Bridge, I could remember 250,000 things but I don't have a secretary, a referee, a general director or a group of people writing them all down for me. We will just take to the pitch at 8.45 at this ground tomorrow and try to play football in the best way possible. But in this press room he's the fucking boss [the exact words: '*el puto jefe, el puto amo*'], the one who knows more than everyone else, so I don't want to spend a moment trying to compete with him.'

He carried on, but let us pause for a moment here to consider a few things. Pep's tone is ice calm, but he was brimming with indignation. Guardiola was offended. Including on a personal level, as we'll see shortly. Ever since Mourinho had first sat on the Real bench in the summer, he had acknowledged the fact that the verbal warfare would be continuous, but he was uninterested in it, letting his rival talk and not giving him the satisfaction of responding to it. This time though he had gone to a new level that had forced him to react: Mourinho had addressed him directly, making it a personal issue. Pep was perfectly aware that Mou was trying to get on his nerves to slow down his tactical reflexes. Normally Barcelona would definitely win, but in a heated climate things are different, and Mourinho, who was aware of this, acted accordingly. The personal attack, however, is an affront to the code of conduct that Guardiola holds dearly, and it was clear he wanted to put an end to it here so that he wouldn't have to be apprehensively looking out for other low blows.

●

AT THE START OF THIS BOOK I MENTIONED A FILM,

The Duellists, which tells the story of a similar rivalry between two Napoleonic officers. At this stage, Guardiola has now taken on the role of d'Hubert in the final scene. After being forced for years to accept Feraud's challenges through a misplaced sense of honour, d'Hubert accepted one last duel, two pistol rounds each to put an end to it once and for all. The duel took place in a ruined castle; Feraud missed his target twice and found himself at point blank range in front of d'Hubert, who had one bullet left. Feraud – who, in terms of his character, as we've already said, is the Mourinho of the story – told him to kill him quickly. But d'Hubert – Guardiola – had another idea: 'You have kept me at your beck and call for 15 years. I shall never again do what you demand of me. By every rule of single combat, your life now belongs to me. Is that not correct? Then I shall simply declare you dead. In all of your dealings with me you will do me the courtesy to conduct yourself as a dead man. I have submitted to your notions of honour long enough. You will now submit to mine.' Pep dreamed that his speech could have the same significance, liberating him forever from a contest he hated. But he didn't hate his interlocutor. He hated his determination to use any weapon available to him, including underhanded acts. If Mourinho would only give him the courtesy of conducting himself as a dead man every time he considered a confrontation, he would be immensely satisfied with that.

●

BUT LET US RETURN TO THE PRESS ROOM IN THE
Bernabéu.

'I will just remind you that we worked together for four years: he knows me, I know him, and that's all I'll say. If he wants to go by things written about what I said after the Copa del Rey that were reported by the media here,' he pointed at the TV cameras again, 'and by the friends of the president, Don Florentino Pérez,' a dramatically formal reference to show he was keeping his distance, 'if that matters more than our friendship...no, not friendship, more than the relationship that we have, that's up to him. He can keep reading Albert [Einstein], or putting his faith in Florentino Pérez's friends and their milkmaid's tales, which you all know about here in Madrid. It's up to him to decide what he wants to do. I'm not going to... I don't have to justify my words, after their victory I simply congratulated Real Madrid because that's what Barcelona does. I congratulated Real Madrid for the cup they had won...' a pause that indicates what comes next should be underlined, 'deservedly, on the pitch, against a good team that I am very proud to represent.' The answer to the first question had finished. Guardiola might have had a more cutting finish, because he had turned towards José's TV camera with the grimaced expression that seemed to say, 'I can't remember if I wanted to say something else', before a signal from Chemi invited him to stop. The only sound was a long hiss of the clicking from all the cameras taking photos to immortalise the historic moment.

Pep Guardiola isn't one of those coaches who, to avoid getting into trouble, only say the most obvious, banal and tedious things. According to his own code of communication, which as we've seen includes never giving exclusive interviews, when he speaks the content should be lavish, full of stories and richly coloured. Maybe it's not as easy to immediately identify the headline that your editor is asking for ('it's eight o'clock, give me an idea of the headline, send me the piece later'), but he is never boring. It is by considering this background that we can truly appreciate the magnitude of what we have just heard, from the caricatured jokes about milkmaids – the media network surrounding Florentino and Real, the 'whites' – to the strong reminder about the four years they had spent together. They aren't friends, as Guardiola pointed out for the avoidance of doubt, but they do know each other, and there was a significant allusion to what was left unsaid, almost as if to say 'don't make me reveal more'. The incident at San Mamés immediately comes to mind: perhaps, after fifteen years, Pep is calling in the debt he feels José owes him after that evening in Bilbao, when his intervention probably prevented him getting beaten up. But that's unlikely; his calm rage appears to be more about calling for a truce. Guardiola doesn't feel as though he has been attacked by Mourinho's words, but rather insulted by them; he is perfectly aware that the marginal offside call against Pedro is a pretext, an excuse to tarnish the sporting image of both himself and Barcelona. There is something more profound in the destabilising tactics of Mou's speech: there is a twisted pleasure in saying that they are all equal, of taking Guardiola out of the group of coaches that don't talk about referees. Pep denies this when he recalls that after the game he complimented Real for their victory, reiterating how deserved it was. And in the end he threw his rival one last lifeline, suggesting that his negative comments weren't the result of his own reasoning, but were instead the influence of a malevolent media, those journalists close to Florentino. The lead milkmaid. It was a verbal ploy to avoid burning all his bridges, but he knew better than anyone how things really were. His last strong message, the true declaration of pride, was the refusal to justify his own comments. In this,

Guardiola showed himself to be absolutely resolute.

For many of the journalists present, used to football matches and not wars, these were 150 seconds of unimaginable intensity. They looked around at each other, and the dozens of expressions caught between surprise and admiration perfectly described the exceptional nature of the day's stories, from Mourinho's bombshell to Guardiola's explosive response. Later on there would be conflicting views in how to read the situation, because like with any great chess match that is interrupted to be continued the next day, some favour a numerical advantage in the number of pieces left, while others favour the primacy of position. Mou hit hard with numerous arguments and examples (numerical advantage), while Pep hit back equally hard and, in maintaining his principles, didn't allow himself to sink to his opponent's level (positional advantage).

There were so many things to talk about over *sobremesas*, but we knew that no one would be sitting down to eat before 11pm – we had to write, and for once it wouldn't be quick – and no one would be finishing much before 2am. The night before a Clásico is one of the longest (and best) nights of the football season.

Naturally there were other questions. Guardiola remained seated for 20 minutes and spoke about a number of other compelling topics. Lu Martin of *El País* – his old friend – asked him about playacting, obviously in reference to the accusations of simulation made by Sergio Ramos on Monday, and he didn't hold back in his reply: 'It's one of *Señor* José's old theories, years ago he convinced his Chelsea players of this and now he's done the same with his Madrid players. I thought since then he would have come up with a different strategy. One other thing: *Señor*

Mourinho has been a part of this club that I represent, and he knows that there are a lot of things that don't work here. A lot of things. But we always try to compete in the best way that we know how, which is by playing good football. He knows this, he learned it here because we helped to develop him into a coach.' Another reminder of Mourinho's origins: you know about Barcelona's values, you developed with us, what has transformed you into our fiercest ideological enemy?

It was then the turn of a colleague who worked for one of the national radio stations. He began by saying that he wanted to be very direct, before asking him if he saw a pattern in the way in which some sections of the media misinterpreted his words. Pep began his reply as an educated person would do – 'I was taught that if someone doesn't understand what I'm saying, it's my fault because I've explained myself badly' – but he quickly swerved towards a topic he had sworn not to touch: explaining what he had said about Pedro's disallowed goal. 'My thoughts were nothing like the wonderful interpretation given to them by the coach of Real Madrid. I simply wanted to say that the referee did very well, given that it was offside by this much,' he indicated a couple of centimetres with his fingers, 'and therefore that the difference between winning and losing was minimal. José can believe me, or he can believe what he reads; my understanding is that he is more interested in believing what he reads.'

Why this change of tone, Pep? Has Mourinho worn you down? Have you had enough? These are fair questions, accurately diagnosing Guardiola's weariness in having to spend so much time dealing with off-field issues. He tried to refute this by changing his tone, but his reply only strengthened the interviewer's case. 'My tone is always the same, you know me, you can check this. What bothers me...Basically, at this point my previous seasons should be taken into consideration as well, given that I'm now finishing my third season with Barcelona. Am I a coach who complains about referees? Am I the type who tries to use their mistakes as an excuse for our defeats? Am I someone who covers up any mistakes that go our way when we win? I know the answer to these, we don't talk about referees here, but I can't fight against those who argue to the contrary.'

In the next part of his answer, addressing what it is that he does for his team, Guardiola fell back slightly into the rhetoric of the *canteranos*, the players he has brought up from the youth team – 12 of them this time – compared to the millions Real had spent on their many star players. It's a debate that is linked to the clubs' differing policies, which certainly provides Barcelona with financial rewards given that they don't need to burden themselves with the sort of outlay like €90 million for Ronaldo, but instead can enjoy developing Leo Messi from the age of 13. It is a given that developing a world class player costs much less than buying the finished article, but there is nonetheless a time when the wage bill of Real's international superstars and of the talented products of La Masia balance each other out. Messi doesn't earn less than Ronaldo, Piqué has roughly the same pay as Sergio Ramos, Iniesta and Di María earn the same. What must be said is that the policy under Laporta and Guardiola was highly oriented towards developing local talent (the Ibra mistake aside), while Rosell and later Bartomeu, by spending large amounts on Neymar and Suarez, pointed the club in a similar direction to Real Madrid.

Guardiola responded to many other journalists in a 25-minute press conference, which is a considerable but not a record duration. He went over many of the same ideas a number of times, translating them into English and Catalan as well, but what he always came back to was the reminder of the institution he represented and the sporting values that inspired Barcelona, and his consequent surprise that these were being denied by a man who should have been perfectly well aware of them given that they had been instilled in him during his four long years at the club. His anger towards him increased with every passing minute, even though, a few answers before, he had offered him the escape route of the 'evil' media, as if the full scale of his culpability was only just dawning on him. When he speaks about Real, in fact, Guardiola isn't able not to express a form of admiring respect. For example, in response to someone who asked him whether the many injuries would affect Barça's perennial attitude to playing attacking football, he said angelically: 'I've come to this stadium many times, as a player and as a coach, and I can guarantee you that if you start off trying to limit the damage then you will be annihilated immediately. That's what the Bernabéu is like: great players urged on by great supporters. You have to play with courage.' Of Mourinho, meanwhile he said that 'this is a coach who has won more than me and who has a unique prestige. On the pitch I try to learn from him every time we play each other, as I do whenever I watch his teams play on TV. Off the pitch, however, I try and learn as little as possible.' A nice strike at his morals. Finally, to the person who observed that he had never seen him be so passionate in the three years he had been Barcelona coach, he replied: 'It's the first time that he has called me Pep, and that he says I've done this and that. So, I have to respond...' Suddenly Chemi realised that he might say something regrettable and put a hand on Guardiola's shoulder, but he brushed it off decisively; he wanted to finish his sentence. 'He accused me of using referees as an excuse, even though I never talk about them...Stamford Bridge? It's true, that evening we got some fortunate decisions. It happens. Last year in San Siro there was a foul on Alves in the box and Milito's goal was offside. I'm saying this for the first time, since they're on José's list. I didn't complain about them then, and I'm not complaining about them now. But if you make a list, it should be complete.'

NINE

WHILE GUARDIOLA WAS TALKING TO THE PRESS,
the players were still finishing their training session on the pitch
in the Bernabéu. After showering, they switched on their phones
as they began to head back up to the team bus to find them
clogged up with enthusiastic messages. Xavi recounted the moment to *Sky Sports* journalist Guillem Balagué, the author of a
fine biography of Guardiola: 'I was impressed when I heard what
Pep did. Shocked. And I liked it. I liked it a lot.' Back in the
hotel, the players rushed back to their rooms in search of a news
channel that was reviewing the press conference. They soon saw
it, and as they called out to each other from their rooms, they
laughed and cheered at the salient moments of Pep's responses,
which were obviously the most controversial ones. Some of the

players' relatives had come to Madrid and were sat down in the lobby, and they could hear the players' excitement before they had even seen them. The afternoon's indignation at Mourinho's accusations had been transformed first into relief, because Pep had finally hit back, and then into enthusiasm, because once the dam had been breached the flood swept everything away with it. Twenty-four hours before a very difficult Champions League semi-final, the team regrouped in the restaurant in high spirits: a situation that would have been unthinkable just a few hours before, and is rare enough as it is. When Guardiola entered the room, accompanied by the film director David Trueba, one of his friends, he received a standing ovation. Every player got to his feet and applauded him for thirty seconds. While he was aware that he had sent a strong message both to the opposition and to his own players, Pep was stunned.

When evening came, a typically cool April evening, the excitement in Madrid was at its peak. That night the Spanish capital was undoubtedly the centre of the football world: the restaurants were full of former players who had come from around the globe to commentate on the big match for their respective TV channels, the best journalists were there too, and wherever you looked you saw a director you knew, a coach, that famously outlandish Mexican journalist who was maybe too caught up in the moment to be taken entirely seriously, friends who you hadn't seen since the last World Cup or European Championships, in accordance with the biennial pattern that governs football's global village. Filippo Ricci, the excellent journalist who reports on Spanish football for *La Gazzetta dello Sport* from Madrid, is the pivot around which everything else revolves. Together with two other top class correspondents, the Englishman Sid Lowe of the *Guardian* and the Argentine Martin Einstein of ESPN Latin America, he hosted *Los Corresponsales*, a trilingual podcast broadcast on YouTube, in which they discuss and analyse the latest news in a wonderfully light-hearted way. As one of the organisers of the football team for foreign journalists stationed in Madrid, there are no doors that aren't open to him. The maître d' of the Argentine restaurant De Maria, for example, frequently goes to watch their games. It so happens that on evenings like this, when people are queuing out the door onto the Calle Felix Boix (which is strategically positioned a few blocks away from the Bernabéu), he opens the private room of the restaurant, which has a TV, to his friends to allow us to work while watching the other semi-final between Schalke and Manchester United, throwing in a glass of wine in the excitement of the day's events and in anticipation of what is to come the next day. Naturally the room is a hive of activity, people are going in and out, some sit and watch the game and take the opportunity to have dinner – it should be the other way round but it's such an informal atmosphere that plates of prosciutto arrive without needing to order them – others are reading through articles, others are drinking more than just the one glass. Sitting next to me is Michael Robinson, a former Liverpool player who, after finishing his career at Osasuna, moved to Madrid and became a notable TV analyst, first on national television and then on Canal+. *Informe Robinson* is one of their most popular programmes. As a man of Irish blood, he's an excellent drinker, and I finished my article with some difficulty while he explained to me – completely uninterested in whether I was following him or not – the differences between Spanish and Italian football. To his left was Santiago Solari, a player who didn't stand out when he was at Real Madrid or Inter, but who has become an unexpectedly brilliant analyst, and writes weekly columns for *El País*. Some years later, when Zidane replaced Rafael Benítez, there was talk that he was the man who Florentino wanted to install alongside the Frenchman, but Zizou made sure his old assistant, David Bettoni, would continue with him in his new adventure. When the curtain, which separates the room from the other customers, was pulled back to allow Ronaldo – *O Fenomeno*, the other one was preparing for the match – it was clear that the night was just getting started. And it wasn't yet one in the morning.

At the same time as the city was enjoying a long night before the big show, the stars of the show itself were struggling to get some sleep. It's always the same on the night before a big game. One could easily cross paths in the hotel corridors with coyotes – as Enzo Bearzot began to call all insomniacs after Marco Tardelli – each one with his own demons, preferring to keep their thoughts to themselves, unlike the old days when games of cards worked as a soporific. Instead, now they just want to be in their own world, the confines of which are normally their headphones that isolate them and their music. Or perhaps a prayer, a message to relatives, or even a chat up line. Everyone has their own way about avoiding thinking about the next day.

Among those who weren't sleeping were the two coaches.

Guardiola stalked across his room, walking up to the window and looking out into the darkness as though it were the bottom of a well. He was convinced his team were technically inferior: he could tell the squad were tired and the injuries to Iniesta and his left-backs were forcing him into solutions that were a far cry from the efficiency of his ideal starting line-up. On the other hand, he had noticed that his response to Mourinho had fully restored Barça's pride, and privately he started to hope that his rival's psychological warfare – this time, perhaps *enemy* is the more apposite term – would turn out to be an own goal: that Mou, through his exaggerations, had motivated Barcelona's players more than Real Madrid's. Modern football's top clubs are packed with quality players, but they are used to looking out for themselves and as such they are groups of professionals who often lack deep-rooted feelings. They have to be able to work with anyone, whether or not the coach is admired or even likeable, and therefore they have to avoid making controversial remarks, because you never know who might be the next coach to take charge. Barcelona's squad made an exception for Mourinho, openly detesting him, which is only natural considering that the Portuguese had decided years earlier (even from his time at Chelsea) to adopt the most controversial, conflicting stance possible to what had once been his club. There was a precise meaning to the standing ovation given to Guardiola in the restaurant: don't torment yourself over getting sucked into Mourinho's little games, we're still proud of you and we're happy that you haven't ignored this one. As a good friend, Estiarte understood that this was the time to support Pep and his decisions more than ever, and that on this occasion he should keep his many doubts about using this opportunity to respond so directly to himself; after the defeat in the Copa del Rey, Iniesta's injury had transformed what was already a difficult match to a very difficult one. Manel was once a great champion and knew the first rule of sport, which is as unfair as it is unavoidable: all that matters is the result, everything else is cast in its shadow. If Barcelona got to the final, Pep's response would be considered brilliant, if Real qualified it would be foolish. But he would tell this to him later. The night before the game was the time for his unconditional support.

A few kilometres away, in the quiet of Valdebebas, Mourinho was unable to sleep either. Guardiola's reply, however strong it was, had clearly been thought through, so while he had succeeded in his plan of involving Pep in a verbal war, he hadn't defeated him. In fact, it was likely that Mourinho was worried that these words ended up inspiring Barcelona, though he never admitted as much. It now remained to be seen if the stress he had induced would be enough to force them to lose focus. Mourinho went over and over his team and his substitutes, aware that if things were to go badly then he would be reproached for keeping Kaká, Benzema and Higuaín on the bench while Pepe and Lass Diarra had played in midfield. But he wouldn't make an exception to his plan, which would see an additional defender playing in midfield – Pepe – and the playmaker – Özil – to be positioned in a more advanced role in place of a forward. The brightest of his stars, Cristiano Ronaldo, had already told him several times that he would prefer a more attacking line-up, but the coach was rightly convinced that the support of Jorge Mendes, their hugely powerful agent, would enable him to deal with the dissent of his most important player. Ronaldo and Mourinho were the most lucrative assets in his portfolio, and up until Madrid the agent had made sure to keep their careers separate, in order not to have all his eggs in one basket. But with the vast expansion of his empire and his 'client' Florentino Pérez's request to do something to stop Barcelona's dominance, Mendes was practically forced to bring his two thoroughbreds together, using himself as a guarantee – he is a very close friend of both of them – to make sure they got along, or at least to find an acceptable *modus vivendi*.

The last player Mourinho had had a conversation with before shutting himself off in his room was Pepe, another of Mendes' clients. The role of the villain which he had been cast in, instructed to be aggressive and underhanded, was a heavy burden to bear, and occasionally Mou was forced to assure him that he would have his full support, whatever happened, whether it was for a new contract or to rebut criticism. Pepe was an excellent centre back both at Porto and at the start of his career in Madrid: the move forward into midfield required him to run much more and have an impact in open play, whereas he and his talents were really more at home in congested areas of the pitch. Pepe was very exposed in midfield, and, moreover, in an area where he would be confronted with Messi's pace, and Mourinho asked him to intimidate rather than commit fouls. International referees would take no notice of Real's prestige, particularly when the other team was an (almost) equally prestigious club, and would give fouls, show yellow cards and send players off. Pepe's job was to run along a tightrope, to incite fear, and therefore stress, without taking too many risks. An incredibly difficult job, but he accepted it without complaint. Pepe is a soldier.

●

THE NEXT DAY, THE DELEGATIONS FROM THE

two clubs' management teams entered the selected *asador* after

1pm for the official lunch, not far from the stadium, and the first course of Iberico ham – the best quality, the better-known serrano is a rip-off for tourists – was served in the cool surroundings of the private room. The newspapers were bursting with pages with news and background stories about the previous day's press conferences, and the directors were looking uncomfortably down at their shoes. Rosell was the first to get a hold of himself, and addressed Pérez directly: 'President, you have to do something to make your coach hold his tongue. We can't allow his controversies to contaminate the clubs and their fans.' Florentino looked at him as though he were being naive, to put it mildly. 'President, you know Mourinho. There's nothing I can do to stop him saying whatever he thinks.'

No censure, then, Mourinho will say 'whatever he thinks.'

The message was clear: right now the coach is the embodiment of all Madridistas exhausted by Barcelona's long period of dominance, and the victory in the Copa del Rey, the first they had achieved since Guardiola arrived, had allowed him unlimited credit. In other words: if we win by creating controversy, then we will create as much controversy as we like. Rosell took note of Pérez's response – which was on the verge of mockery – and the lunch silently drew to a quick conclusion. The traditional *sobremesas*, sweets and liqueurs, which allow friends to chat at the end of a meal, weren't even served.

There is no small-talk here.

There are no friends here.

●

EVEN THOUGH IT IS VERY LARGE, THE PRESS BOX in the Bernabéu isn't capable of holding everyone who applies for media accreditation. There were over a thousand requests, a record number for a club match, and as a result the press office partly arranged the seating by nationality. For example, all the Italians were sent up to the fifth tier, which is much less comfortable (there are no desks to write on or monitors to watch replays: they were seats which are normally put on public sale for La Liga games), but the selection criteria was faultless. Italy wasn't involved in any way. In this exhibition of world football, the Argentines had Messi, Mascherano and Di María, the Portuguese had Mou and Ronaldo, the Germans had Özil, the Brazilians had Alves and Marcelo, the French had Diarra, and so on, and therefore journalists from those countries had the best seats. And people wonder why we complain that we're a bit hard on our players sometimes...

It takes a little longer for the spring sun to set over the stadium up on the fifth tier, a great spot to sit and close your eyes, up until the moment the teams come out onto the pitch. Mourinho waited for Guardiola at the exit of the tunnel that leads out from the dressing rooms so that he could quickly shake his hand and turn back towards his dugout: the handshakes were a mere greeting, nothing more. That said, Mourinho would certainly not have minded the fact that, as the two shook hands, he was in the higher, more dominant position.

In a stadium like the Bernabéu, full of history and exciting memories for anyone who loves the game of football, the final few minutes before a big match kicks off are the most exhilarating, because it generates such heightened stimuli in what is an already beautiful atmosphere that it's almost impossible for the brain to take it all in. You have to open your heart to it as well, that part of our personality entrusted with receiving and developing deep feelings, and once those feelings are inside you, they change, develop, transform, explode. It is the fans singing *Hala Madrid* who begin to communicate the pride and prestige of the biggest club in the world, then comes the film on the stadium's big screen as the teams wait to enter the pitch – staring silently and grimly at each other through the metal grill – before they line up for the Champions League anthem. It is everything that has made Real fans fall in love with the club, and everything that inspires admiration and respect for them across the world, all summed up in three minutes. The sublime voice of Luciano Pavarotti singing *Nessun Dorma* is the backdrop for the various clips on the big screen, first in black and white, then in colour, of the great champions who have worn this shirt across the ages: there are goals from Alfredo Di Stéfano, Gento, Ferenc Puskás, then from Emilio Butragueño, Hugo Sánchez and Míchel, then Raúl, Predrag Mijatović, Zidane and the Brazilian Ronaldo, before it comes to Sergio Ramos, some saves from Casillas, Cristiano passionately celebrating every goal, whether it's important or not. Tonight though, some quick-thinker has added the goal that Ronaldo scored in Valencia on Wednesday to the video together with a frame of Casillas lifting the cup in the Plaza de Cibeles, just before Pavarotti's final notes sound over the last image of the Bernabéu shining like a beacon of light in the darkness. The roar that meets the end of the film, allowing the Champions League music to begin, is the prelude to a storm: Merengue scarves are waved in all four stands, creating the effect of white foam on the waves of a stormy sea. This is it, the moment of the height of Real Madrid's power in this story. The moment in which the enormous value of their current squad connects with the wonders of the past. The line of Catalans shortens a bit, everyone standing a bit closer to the captain Puyol, who is definitely not in the best physical condition, but on nights like this is he is at least as essential, if not more, than Messi. 500 Culé fans are supporting them from a position high up to our right in the area allotted to them by UEFA: seen up on high, impossible to hear even though you can see they are singing their songs, they look like an outpost of abandoned men

TEN

KICK-OFF. THERE WAS A TACTICAL SURPRISE contained in Real's ultra-physical team: Pepe was in midfield, but playing on the left rather than centrally like he had in Valencia. Mourinho left Xabi Alonso in front of the defence to exploit his range of passing and, theoretically, to ensure his key man wouldn't get involved in a potentially fatal duel against Messi's pace. Pepe's mission was instead to stick close to an equally important but much more static player, Xavi, whose importance to the Catalans' build up play had doubled in the absence of Iniesta. Fate has gifted me one creative player's absence – Mourinho thought – I'll bury the other one under a pile of cement. Pepe needed to help Di María to contain Dani Alves' bursts forward as well, while on the other side Lass, apart from closing down

145

Busquets and Keita, also needed to keep an eye on the wing in case Puyol tried his luck coming forward. These were all defensive tactics, difficult for a Real Madrid side playing at the Bernabéu to stomach, but so be it: the three centre forwards – remember the debates of the previous autumn about 'cats' and 'dogs'? – were all on the bench together with Kaká, the only one who could afford a smile after his flying visit to see his new born daughter. There was no one playing in a central role because Ronaldo preferred to take up wider positions, while the roles of Özil on the right and Di María on the left oscillated between containing and attacking. Add to this an initial caution from Marcelo, who is normally almost an extra forward down the left hand side, and you have a picture of a Real side who were, to say the least, very respectful of their opposition. Mourinho had already made his surprise move of starting aggressively in Valencia: to replicate the strategy in a two-legged affair may have seemed too risky to him, or perhaps simply too predictable.

The fans in the Bernabéu held their collective breath as they watched the game, and generally they weren't particularly taken with the team's very prudent approach. They were hungry for another victory after the triumph in Valencia had broken years of Catalan domination. They hated everything about that domination, from the elegance of Guardiola – who was wearing a tie unlike Mou, who had chosen a dark shirt under a grey suit – to their insistence on playing possession football. After a few minutes, exasperated by the Blaugrana defence's early passes, Ronaldo began a difficult but spectacular exercise: he went chasing after the ball as it rolled, quickly but not that quickly due to the long, dry grass, between Piqué, Puyol and Xavi. He needed to have lightning pace if he was to succeed, as well as inexhaustible stamina and obviously the help of his team-mates. Ronaldo set off like a wild beast in pursuit of Piqué, and after failing to intercept the ball he changed course for Puyol, who got there a metre ahead of him, his face flushed from the effort, and found Xavi, who then had three metres of space (and time) to weigh up the next pass. After failing for a third time Ronaldo stopped to catch his breath, and only then did he realise that he had been the only one in pursuit of the ball, because his closest team-mate was 20 metres further back, not only behind the ball but also behind the halfway line. An angry look crossed his face; Cristiano yelled and gestured frantically at the crowd, who took his side by whistling the rest of the team's defensive attitude. Not that it would make Mourinho change his plan in the slightest: there was still plenty of time for that.

For their part, Barcelona weren't much more proactive or spectacular. Puyol wasn't leaving his position at left back, at most he would move slightly more centrally when Alves advanced down the opposite wing, as the defence rearranged itself into a back three. There was no *salida lavolpiana* – both full-backs could advance simultaneously when Busquets dropped back between the centre backs: a move invented by the Argentine coach Ricardo La Volpe, hence the name – which was no surprise if he didn't have the energy to get back quickly enough. Guardiola was coming off the back of the defeat in Valencia and had taken a heavy blow with Iniesta's injury: he knew he could go for the kill in the Camp Nou. While he was trying to spark Messi into life, he was carefully judging how best to do so. Up to this point, Leo hadn't played a major part in the series. It's certainly true

that Mourinho had paid particular attention to him as he prepared for each match, aware of how he had been able to tactically
cage him a year before during the semi-final with Inter. Other
top class coaches had dedicated themselves to trying to reduce
the creative genius' impact on games and only succeeded for a
few minutes. José, on the other hand, seemed to have a sort of
indescribable power over him, because while he never directly attacked him – the reason for which comes from reading between
the lines: we're both at early stages of our careers, who knows
whether we'll work together one day – he was often able to make
him lose his composure; his every move was anticipated, and he
found himself frequently surrounded by defenders. There was
one tiny detail that was different this time though; perhaps too
small to be important, perhaps it would be telling. The tensions,
including personal ones, between the two teams' players were
at fever pitch by this point, the pre-match handshakes were an
exhibition of stony looks and rushed acknowledgements, including between many individuals from the same national teams; it
was a formality that was more akin to two boxers menacingly
facing each other before the first bell than two football teams.
The only exception was Messi himself who, when passing his
friend and international team-mate Di María, stopped for a
moment and gave him a reciprocated kiss on the cheek. Maybe
it was a sign. Unlike his team-mates, completely caught up in
the heat of battle, Leo was able to compartmentalise this within
himself, in a space that wasn't governed by stress but by deep-
rooted sensations and feelings. If that's where he kept his way of
playing football, tonight was the night to find it.

As both super clubs treated each other with visible respect –

which, at this level, is the prelude to fear – their attempts to score in the first 10 minutes were mainly speculative. Xavi finished off a sequence of five headers with a volley from 20 metres, Ronaldo's left-footed shot from a similar distance was hopeful, a shot across the bows that – like the previous effort – was the same as a check in a poker game: I'm here, over to you. They were opening salvos, the signs of a storm still only on the horizon, but even so any shot on goal might be punished by the slightest lapse of concentration, be it from the goalkeeper or not. 10 minutes had gone when David Villa decided that it was time to take the initiative and take a shot with more conviction: he reached the right hand side of the box, cutting in towards the left followed by Marcelo and Pepe, and when he saw an opportunity he fired a left-footed shot not just towards goal but aiming for the far corner. The ball bounced in front of the diving Casillas but he calmly watched – or at least appearing to be calm – the shot go past the post. Three minutes later Messi went on his first run, bearing down on the penalty area by playing *pared* – as the Spanish call short triangular passes that are so perfectly played they look like they have bounced off a wall (a *pared*) – with Xavi, but after moving the ball out to the left, Pedro's cross was cut out by the Madrid defence. Leo's second dribble forward was infinitely more dangerous: in the 25th minute, he played an acute pass to find Xavi in the box – who knows what the playmaker was doing there – who forced Casillas into a somewhat desperate save. Real's control of the game was fast becoming a distant memory.

The third shot from Xavi, over the bar this time, revealed one of Guardiola's tactics: while remaining on the right hand side, he was playing 10 metres further up the pitch in order to play closer to the forwards, in a similar position to the one usually taken up by Iniesta on the other side of the pitch. It was a wise move, because Iniesta's replacement, Keita, is a more defensive player: better to keep him 10 metres further back, thus giving Xavi the space, if it was not occupied by Messi, to assume a role that could be defined as a *trequartista*. Real tried to respond through set pieces: Pepe rose highest to meet a long ball from Xabi Alonso, but his header ended up in the hands of Valdes. Albiol had jumped next to Pepe, while Sergio Ramos was putting pressure on the goalkeeper: with all his forwards on the bench, the defenders were leading Mourinho's assault.

A little later on, towards half time, Ronaldo decided to send everyone – friends and foes alike – a more dangerous statement of intent: he was in almost the same position as he had been when he took his previous effort, but this time his right-footed shot was unleashed with more power, and it was a substantially quicker shot. Valdes took no chances; he didn't try to hold it and simply beat it away with his fists, but only to where Özil was lurking: the German took what was essentially the first and last touch of his lifeless match by taking a gamble on the goalkeeper being slightly out of position and trying a shot. He connected poorly with it, although the linesman's offside flag indicated that play had already stopped. Ronaldo visibly exhaled. His team-mates had nicknamed him 'El Ansia' due to the state of perennial anxiety he trained and played in, his obsessive attention to detail, and his conviction that others not only didn't have this same attention but that sometimes they didn't even have the bare minimum. It isn't a good nickname, but rather it's a form of trash talking towards the Portuguese, the habit – well-established in professional American sports – of winding up those who are close to you, whether they are a rival or a team-mate, by insulting them (or giving them a death stare, as Cristiano does) in order either to hurt them or to motivate them. It's said that Kobe Bryant was a master at this.

Stark's half time whistle came after an innocuous cross from Pedro ended up in Casillas' arms, and it was curious to see the opposing responses from the two teams: while the Catalans calmly headed towards the tunnel, jogging at their usual pace, every Real player, from Casillas to Ronaldo, ran off at the double, clearly following an instruction given to them before the game. White shirts rapidly disappeared off the Bernabéu pitch, leaving those in Blaugrana placidly heading back towards the dressing room behind them. There was a strong contrast in their differing speeds: Real seemed to have reached the point at which they needed to implement the next phase of their game plan, but Barcelona hadn't. The feeling was that there was a small but indisputable positional advantage, which was obviously that the Catalans had come through 45 minutes in their opponents' stadium unscathed. There was no time to think about this, though, because a mass brawl was breaking out. As they were leaving the pitch Real Madrid's players crossed paths with Pinto, the reserve goalkeeper who had started in Valencia, who had the brilliant idea to reproach Arbeloa for an obstruction he had committed on Pedro shortly before, and which had cost him a (unnecessary) yellow card: words were quickly exchanged, Ramos was immediately involved, the Catalan bench rallied behind Pinto, and while Karanka abandoned the squabbling players with a disgusted expression, the ex-full back Chendo – now a Real official – was in the middle of it trying to restore order, and a couple of security staff had to intervene to help calm things down. After the referee had arrived on the scene and briefly consulted his assistants, he pulled out a red card to send Pinto off (though Barcelona still had eleven players on the pitch, they were now without a substitute goalkeeper). It must have been the right decision, because it brought the chaos to a quick conclusion.

If the third Clásico of the series was a dark raincloud, this incident was just a brief shower – the skies remained dark overhead.

Mourinho and Guardiola got up from their positions on the bench after just two minutes of the second half – as though their seats were burning hot and to be sat on them for twenty more seconds would have been too much to endure – to resume stalking their respective technical areas. This sort of game is like one of Rembrandt's famous paintings, the *Night Watch*, where lots of perfectly depicted figures fill the scene with their individual stories, which when put together create the whole. Despite being very close together, not more than ten metres apart, and despite hearing exactly what the other was saying to his players, Mou and Pep didn't talk to each other, they didn't interact at all except for a few fleeting glances, which were quickly averted as soon as their eyes met. But the duellists were there for all to see, and watching them from behind gave the impression of a carefully-crafted choreography, because their movements to follow the ball were perfectly synchronised, moving from the very left to the centre of their technical areas, then to the very right when it was Barça who were on the attack. Mourinho was dishevelled, looking like a Salzburgian orchestral conductor; Guardiola was composed at the start but became increasingly agitated, like the head of mission control at NASA. Houston, we have a problem. Adebayor had come on for Özil, and while it made Real Madrid still less creative, now they had a target to aim for up front.

Mourinho kept Real in a 4-3-3 shape, putting the Togolese in the centre with Cristiano on the right and Di María on the left. The first notable move came from a long ball, which Ronaldo decisively attacked after Piqué and Puyol had hesitated and clumsily failed to clear. The Portuguese trapped the ball as its momentum took him out wide, he turned virtually on the byline but found three players between him and the goal: Puyol was in front of him, Piqué slightly behind him to cover the goal, and Valdes placed in between the two to close what gap was left. Cristiano shot anyway, hitting the Barça captain, who had reacted incredibly quickly after ending up on the floor following the mistake with Piqué. With the game being so tense right from the start, it was now becoming increasingly heated, and the first major decision came eight minutes into the second half. It was a (justified) yellow card for Sergio Ramos, who was guilty of fouling Messi; Ramos had been a yellow card away from a suspension, and would therefore be suspended for the second leg. Mourinho was seething. Not at the referee – it was unquestionably a booking – but at his defender; he had put a lot of trust in him and would need Ramos at the Camp Nou, and how.

In general, it could be argued that Real were playing too aggressively and Barcelona were protesting too animatedly. The game was at boiling point and every time the referee blew his whistle, numerous players contested the decision, shoving and insulting each other in a manner that threatened to escalate at any point. Fuses were now incredibly short, and you could feel that Stark – on the verge of losing control of the game – might be about to put his foot down to reassert his authority. And indeed he did, in the 61st minute. As he tried to recover a lost ball, Pepe went in high on Dani Alves, who collapsed screaming to the ground and clutching his ankle as though he had been shot. It really was a bad challenge. Followed by two sets of players yelling at him, Stark distanced himself from the incident to speak to his assistant, but there was no real consultation between them. He pulled out the red card and showed it to an incredulous Pepe. At that moment the Bernabéu exploded with anger, producing a sound that I've never heard before, a mix of fury, frustration, hatred, rancour and injustice. Immediately surrounded by TV cameras, Mourinho's jaw dropped, looking like someone who is so astonished by what he's seen he cannot believe his eyes. Suddenly Puyol was next to him, and incredibly the two began talking to each other; the player was clearly signalling 'come on, you're exaggerating' while the coach, taking him by the arm, replied 'he didn't even touch him'. Watching a number of replays, it seems that Mou was right, because Alves had anticipated the challenge: he had moved his foot out of the way of Pepe as he thundered in, who always remained – as far as can be told by watching replays – a few centimetres away from making contact. There is no denying that the challenge was particularly violent, the classic orange card, but given the situation, Barça had good cause to accuse Real of aggressive conduct, while Real would never tire of accusing Barça of simulation. Even in the first half, Busquets, typically, had feigned being elbowed by Marcelo but the referee hadn't been fooled by it.

Mourinho couldn't resist the temptation to sarcastically give the thumbs up to the fourth official, even winking at him, for which Stark sent him to the stands, effectively sending him off. Pepe was laughing as he left the pitch, the classic reaction of someone who has screwed up but wants to demonstrate not only that he believes he is innocent, but that he is in fact the victim. Mou sat in the first row behind the dugout, in a seat behind an orange gate, and understandably he told a photographer who had the courage to ask him to make the handcuff gesture he had once made at Inter to go to hell, which would have been particularly appropriate. From then on he would give instructions to the loyal Rui Faria, who would pass them on to Karanka. The Bernabéu, an immense crowd of people with a single personality, held its breath, livid in the hope that at this point Real would know how to protect the 0-0 result and go to the Camp Nou for the final showdown. But there were still thirty more long minutes to go.

Xavi was the first Catalan to smell blood. He pushed still further forward – while Real were reorganising into a 4-3-2 with Di María pulled back into midfield – and brought Villa and Pedro into play, who had been alternating up until now: the former had been quietly impressive, active in the final third, but the latter had been almost invisible, and would in fact be replaced in the 71st minute by Afellay. The dénouement was not far away. Ronaldo tried to put his team in front from a free kick, but as the ball sailed high over the bar there was the distinct feeling that the game was not destined to go his way.

It's the 77th minute.

Xavi is a dynamo who has found the secret of perpetual motion. He offered the ball to Messi to dribble towards Casillas' goal, but he was crowded out by the number of defenders and gave the ball back to him. Maradona once said of Jorge Burruchaga that 'giving him the ball is like putting it in the bank', and the same could be said of Xavi, with the additional benefit that doing so would be a good investment. He doesn't just keep hold of what you've given him, but will give it back to you with added value. He held onto the ball in a central position, waiting for the right moment to pass it back to Leo, but suddenly he had a moment of inspiration: out wide, Afellay only had Marcelo in front of him. He passed to the Dutchman, who went past the slightly tired Brazilian with ease. He created half a metre of space for himself, and that was enough. His low cross went past Albiol, and even he was reacting slower than in the first half, and arrived in the centre, where Messi held off Ramos' desperate lunge to turn the ball past Casillas.

The goal was scored below the Catalan supporters, celebrating high above in the top tier, and, in the midst of loud Madridista whistles and abuse, Messi looked up at them, pointed to the badge on his shirt, and smiled as though it was the end of a nightmare. He pointed at Afellay too, who, although he couldn't know at the time, had just played the most important pass of his otherwise forgettable spell at Barcelona. Real's defenders looked despondent, while Mourinho didn't even get up from his seat, scowling as he continued to watch his enemies' celebrations. Guardiola clenched his fists with delight, but a moment later he composed himself again and called over Mascherano to pass on his tactical instructions for the final quarter of an hour. It appeared to be over, but the memory of the first Clásico in La Liga, the first of the quadruple header, called for caution: twelve days before Real had been able to turn the tide despite their numerical inferiority.

But the initial assumption was the correct one: there was no reaction at all from the Real bench. Mourinho didn't move a muscle, not caring that Kaká, Higuain and Benzema were itching to get on the pitch to try and turn things round. His mind was working angrily to compose what he would say in what would have to be a flawless press conference, when he would have to answer both to what Pep had said the day before and to what had just happened on the pitch. It's possible that, at 0-1, part of his brain was still thinking about the second leg and the difficult task of turning the tie around without Pepe and Sergio Ramos. But when Messi's incredible goal made it 0-2 – in the 87th minute – any lingering thoughts of still reaching the final disappeared, and effectively defending his own image was the only thing he now hoped to achieve in what remained of a disastrous evening.

And what an incredible goal it was. In the same way that Diego Maradona felt almost obligated to score the best goal in history against England in 1986 to make up for the Hand of God, the infamous goal that put Argentina in front, Leo Messi, who certainly wouldn't escape the media storm coming up, decided to give added weight to the argument that Barcelona deserved to go through purely on the basis of their style of football. Stood with the ball at his feet in midfield, he studied the opposition's defensive position and, giving the ball to Busquets who touched it back to him, he set off to go and score the goal of the season.

The Rosario-born superstar strode forward in a supreme display of two of his best qualities: his pace and his agility. With Lass and Xabi trailing in his wake, Leo reached the edge of the box with the ball glued to his foot, sailed past Albiol who was hopelessly static and swept the ball with his right foot past Casillas into the opposite corner, before either Sergio Ramos or Marcelo could close him down. Iker complained at Ramos, which was a mistake because the path Messi took to get into the box should have been guarded by Albiol, while Leo ran towards the corner flag where the first player to arrive and embrace him was the substitute Gabi Milito, while Guardiola celebrated before taking a long swig of water from the bottle he always had at his side, like a student on an InterRail. Now it really was effectively over. Numerous Real players went up to remonstrate with Stark at full time, who meanwhile was shaking the hands of the Catalan players. But standing at the foot of the stairs leading inside was Rui Faria, spitefully commenting as the opposition went past him 'go and get changed in the referees' dressing room, you're on the same team.' Puyol, Piqué and the others resisted the provocation, telling the Portuguese assistant to stay on his side of the metal grill, but when Rui Faria 'ordered' Pepe to get his own back, he threw himself into a group of players and was quickly knocked down by Puyol. It was the trigger for another fight, this time between players, and before police and stewards were able to separate the protagonists, more than one relationship was irreversibly affected, proof that it is impossible for everything to stay on the pitch when a rivalry is so poisonous. Arbeloa accused Pedro and Busquets of being divers, and ever since the Castilian full back has shown on numerous occasions that there are few who despise Barcelona more than him (even though he played with many of the Catalan side at the 2010 World Cup and the Euros in 2012). Piqué and Ramos' relationship was irretrievably broken, which hurt Vicente Del Bosque particularly badly, given that he had no other centre-back pairing that combined as well as them: the two didn't even speak to each other at the 2014 World Cup, with obvious consequences for the team's performance. We've already noted that the most surprising change of perspective towards the Catalans was Xabi Alonso's, who had been critical of Mourinho, but who was now almost excessively behind the coach's methods. Even Xavi and Casillas, practically childhood friends given that they had gone through all the Spanish youth sides together before playing for la Roja, could hardly look at each other.

With calm restored, Guardiola briskly told everyone who wasn't a member of his coaching team to get out of the dressing room. Before he spoke he ensured that the door was closed and that someone was guarding the entrance. 'I congratulate you for what you've been able to do and for what you've done with all my heart. I'm very proud of you.' His players roared in approval, but their noisy celebrations didn't last long, as at Barajas the plane to take them back to Barcelona was already starting its engines.

On the opposite side of the metal grill, in the Real dressing room, José Mourinho was also fairly concise. 'I'm outraged by what's happened. It's typical UEFA bias towards Barcelona, I'm going to call them out on it in the press room. You must do the same in the mixed zone. Go, talk to the TV and the newspapers, make sure everyone understands what the referee has taken away from us.' The final declaration of war would follow soon after, a few minutes later. Mourinho knew that a lot of journalists were still in the stands, finishing their articles about the game. And he wanted maximum coverage for what he was about to say.

'I didn't say anything to the official, I just gave him the thumbs up after Pepe's red card, nothing more, I didn't applaud him. And he sent me off.'

His first answer to a journalist's question was the perfect launch pad. Mourinho was deathly calm, carefully weighing up every word, and it was clear that he'd spent the final minutes of the game preparing his speech in general terms and was now trying to give it the most forceful possible form by limiting himself to the finer details. He had a dark shirt on underneath his grey suit, his hair was tidy though uncombed, and you had the feeling he had just punched a wall, flushing angrily but with more pain yet to be expressed.

'If I told you or UEFA how I'm feeling now or what I'm thinking, my career as a coach would be over. So instead, I'll just ask a question that I hope can be answered, one way or the other. Why?' The word is divided in two in Spanish – *por qué?* – and with the rhythm of a rapper José repeated it a number of times, associating it with various referees who, in his opinion, had helped Barcelona in recent years. '*Por qué* Ovrebo? *Por qué* De Bleeckere? *Por qué* Busacca? *Por qué* Frisk? *Por qué* Stark? *Por qué?*' Mourinho knew each of the incriminating officials' names by heart, and went through them one by one as if he had a dossier on each of them on the table in front of him. 'Why does the same thing happen in every semi-final?'

He was about to take a revolutionary step in his communication strategy: to pay tribute to the opposition's quality, which was clearly in order firstly to accentuate the referee's crimes, and subsequently to directly cast aspersions on Guardiola. 'We're talking about an absolutely fantastic football team, and so that none of you misinterpret me or say that I didn't say it, we're talking about a fantastic football team.' Mourinho has rarely complimented Barcelona's style of play. In fact he rarely even mentions it, not even this time, thus adhering to a basic rule of communication: by expressly mentioning something you make it visible, by not mentioning it you make it much less visible, and by mangling its name in an apparently sincere way you destroy it completely, which implies that you are so superior you don't even know the name of what's beneath you – a tool that Mourinho uses time and time again.

'I asked myself why try to decide this contest in the first game, we could have been here for three hours and it would still have been 0-0. Or perhaps not, we would have been on a threat if we had brought on Kaká for Lassana, which I was preparing to do... Either way, the strategy I implemented wouldn't have allowed us to lose. Why? I don't understand.'

Mourinho was in full flow, he didn't need questions to follow his exceedingly able train of thought: the reference to bringing on Kaká anticipated the obvious question that, regardless of the referee, Real's approach to playing at home in the first leg had been too cautious. It was just a question of time; he was already thinking about putting Kaká on for the finale: his mental strategy was worthy of *Ocean's Eleven*.

It was now time for another gem in the Portuguese's dialectical mosaic, the hypotheses he threw out to try and answer his own *por qué*. The first one was his masterstroke, because it aimed to bring everyone – and there were many – who didn't support the often overwhelming rhetoric of *buonismo* and political correctness over to his side.

'I don't know if it's the UNICEF publicity,' Mou indicated where the shirt sponsor's name was written: Barcelona didn't have a sponsor, but paid UNICEF so that they could promote their noble cause, 'I don't know if it's the power of Mr Villar [the president of the Spanish Football Federation, who should be neutral in a Clásico] in the offices of UEFA, I don't know if they're nicer people, I don't...I don't...I don't know. I don't understand. Congratulations to a fantastic football team, as I always say, but congratulations for all the other power that you have, because it must have been very difficult to get it. They've succeeded where others don't have a chance. They banned Drogba and Bosingwa at Chelsea, at Inter, where we achieved a miracle by succeeding on our own, Thiago Motta was banned for the final, they banned Wenger and Nasri at Arsenal, and tonight they ban me. All I can do is leave this question in the air and hope that one day I'll get an answer. The referee sent me off, gave me a red card, I shouldn't even be here, but I hope one of you can tell me why. He invented fouls, he opened the game up for them when he sent off Pepe, because they were only able to solve the tactical problems they hadn't workout out how to resolve when we went down to ten men. In the second game, obviously, obviously, it will turn out to be impossible to turn this result around. They have to get to the final and they will get to the final, full stop. I can't understand why this sort of team needs to be helped so obviously, in a way that everyone can see. Football should be simple, with a set of rules that should be the same for everyone so that the best team wins, or the team that deserves to. Today's game should have been 0-0, in the second leg Barcelona would probably have deservedly won, and we would sportingly have accepted it. But like this...Why would you want to influence a game that would otherwise have finished 0-0? Only the referee can answer that, but we know he won't answer: now he'll go back home, because he doesn't have to give explanations to anyone. I...' The overly musical ringtone of someone's mobile interrupts his last sentence. 'Forget it.'

The first storm is over.

Mourinho's diatribe – which can be judged from many angles, but was undoubtedly first class – wasn't just about putting the responsibility for the result entirely on Stark, or more generally about identifying a phantom lobby of UEFA referees to explain years of Barcelona success. The real thrust behind it came from the great speech that Guardiola had made the previous day in the same press room, which had given his side the psychological advantage, which could be considered to be like an away goal in the sense that the verbal battleground had always been Mou's favoured terrain. After the tactical defeat on the pitch – regardless of Pepe's red card, Barça had played like the home side and Real like a provincial away side – the very least he wanted was to regain his advantage in the media that he had lost the previous day. But Mourinho's strategy was predictable, given that he always presses the same buttons; to sustain it, therefore, he had to redouble his efforts yet again and ramp up the controversy to unsustainable levels.

'Should Madrid consider themselves out already?' The second question of the press conference seemed to surprise Mourinho, who after a moment's hesitation said yes with a voice that didn't seem his, almost in falsetto. But he recomposed himself instantly. 'Yes. We'll go there with all our pride, showing maximum respect for our world of football. It's our world even if sometimes...it disgusts me. We'll have to go there without Pepe, who didn't do anything, without Ramos, who didn't do anything, without the coach, who won't be able to sit on the bench, and with a result that is practically impossible to overcome. And if by any chance we succeed in scoring a goal, slightly opening the semi-final up again, they'll kill us once again. Tonight showed that we don't have a chance, and I still have to ask myself why. Why don't they allow other teams to play against them? I don't understand.' A disgusted grimace accompanied this last remark, repeated for the umpteenth time.

The third question concerned his team, but Mourinho was too savvy to let the journalist – who suffice to say wasn't friendly towards him – finish formulating his question. 'Of course, let's talk about the team. It was a team that considered the various stages of a game, and each of their different organisational needs. We got through the first phase in which you mustn't concede, in which you have to be compact and play deep, as we did the other two games. Then, at a set time, by changing our shape and bringing on a number 9, the situation changes. Later on, we can also add a number 10 to play behind the three forwards. This is what tactics is about when trying to play for a 0-0 draw, but you can also try and win it when the opposition get frustrated. You can lose as well, obviously, but the most logical conclusion is that it will be 0-0. This was a plan the referee prevented us from implementing, and I'll ask you again: why? Why did he send Pepe off? Why were we denied four penalties at Chelsea? Why was Thiago Motta sent off? Why Robin van Persie? Why? Where does their power come from? It should be about power on the pitch, and of course they have that too. Why? Winning must taste differently when you win like that. You have to be an awful person not to sense a difference between winning normally and winning in the last minute with a handball. I know exactly what Chelsea supporters went through, even though I wasn't there, and I know exactly what Inter supporters went through before we achieved a miracle, and I know exactly what the people of Madrid are going through now.'

Mourinho was dropping these bombshells into a stunned silence. A few minutes after the end of a big match, the press room in a stadium like the Bernabéu is one of the most noisy and chaotic places in the world, with telephones ringing, TV cameras being moved around, the chatter of journalists, microphones crackling, people going in and out, grabbing officials to ask them which restaurants are still open. This time though, as Mou continued to express his thoughts – their importance was immediately apparent, especially when considering the scale of the number of people involved: it's Real-Barça, after all – it was like a nuclear bomb going off, and there were only two things that could be heard: the tap of keyboards from people typing on their laptops, to send them off as soon as Mou left the room, and the scribble of pens from those writing in their notebooks, who had the luxury of 20 minutes to put their articles together at the end. So, by now he had said everything he wanted to say, right?

Not quite.

'Look,' he said, addressing an imaginary journalist, no one was asking him a direct question this time, 'I want to be frank as I always am. For me, this isn't a tragedy. I'm not that sad, I don't feel that frustrated. Tomorrow is another day, what matters now is going to see my fantastic family waiting for me at home, football comes after them. The only thing that concerns me is not being able to answer why. If the people of Barcelona are honest people...Because they know exactly why. They have a very strong team, but they also know that what I've said is really happening. OK, for them it's simple, they'll carry on like this. They can hide, but...the Catalans are great people, for sure, I know many Catalans and I have friends there...OK, now they're celebrating, 'we're going to Wembley', but they know that winning like that isn't the same. We've won a final [the Copa del Rey] and we knew how to win. We celebrated it with our minds at ease, and that's why Real Madrid is a great club.'

Did he think that the previous day's comments, both his and Guardiola's, had influenced the referee by inflaming the atmosphere too much? It was a very direct question; Mourinho grimaced and started his reply with a quick 'no'. But he picked his words as if he was still considering it. 'I didn't think the atmosphere was too intense. I commented on the words of...Josep Guardiola,' some in the room sniggered, 'and I had the right to do so because they were strange comments, which criticised a good performance from a referee. Josep Guardiola replied to me and he was free to do so. He brought in a bit of politics and I didn't like that, politics and football don't go well together, but that was his decision. I think the conditions were normal and the referee should have been able to handle them normally, but he didn't. When we were denied a penalty against Lyon, I thought, 'OK, he didn't see it', but what happened tonight was absolutely incredible.'

Javi Tamames, the press officer, signalled that it was the turn of the journalist from *Catalunya Ràdio*. Mourinho narrowed his eyes and nodded, because he knew that her question would give him a parting shot. Referring to Guardiola's comments, she asked if Barcelona had just won his Champions League. He abruptly cut her off: 'I've won two Champions Leagues, both on the pitch, and with two teams that weren't Barcelona. The first was with Porto, who come from a country where teams don't normally win the Champions League, the second was with Inter, who hadn't won it for fifty years and weren't one of the favourites. In both cases we won it with a lot of hard work, a lot of effort, a lot of difficulty and a lot of pride. Josep Guardiola is a fantastic coach, as I've said before, but I would be ashamed of the Champions League that he won, because he won it with the scandal at Stamford Bridge, and if he wins it again this year, it will be with the scandal at the Bernabéu. So I hope and wish that one day, he gets the chance of winning a proper Champions League, because Guardiola deserves it', miming the Champions League trophy, 'you win the Champions League by earning it, and when everything is normal. I hope he does because I respect him as a coach, he's very good, and I respect him as a person, because we worked together for four years and he was always very nice towards me. There was absolutely no lack of respect in what I said yesterday, I thought I could be familiar with him by calling him Pep, but apparently not, OK, he's Josep Guardiola, if he wants he's *Señor* Josep Guardiola, that's fine. Either way I respect him a lot, I hope he wins a brilliant, clean Champions League one day.'

Javi pointed at his watch, and no one complained. Everyone's notepads are full.

'*Gracias.*'

Mourinho got up, walked past the press officer and went through the door, while a shocked UEFA official looked on.

•

GUARDIOLA ENTERED THE ROOM A COUPLE OF minutes afterwards, seemingly relaxed even if he must clearly have been highly agitated as a result of the adrenaline of the recently finished match combined with his disgust at Mourinho's comments – the outline of which, at least, he had certainly been told. But Pep had promised himself that the previous day's press conference, the 'fucking boss' one, would be the only time he allowed himself to directly address his rival. He said very little before moving away from the microphones, and when he was asked about the referee's decisions that evening he replied with a barrage of 'I don't know' and 'I can't comment on that'. Other than the touching compliments he paid to Messi – 'he's only 23 years old, 23, and he's already the third highest goalscorer in Barcelona's history. We're all extraordinarily lucky to be able to work with him' – the comment that stuck out was his praise for Madrid's history. Naturally it's impossible to know how much was spontaneous and how much it was inspired by Mourinho's defeatism about his chances of reaching the final. But it's curious that it was the opposition coach, not Real's own coach, who gave them encouragement. 'A club that has won nine Champions League titles never gives a tie up for lost. The second leg will be difficult, we'll have to get a lot of rest in the next few days to recover our strength, and then we'll have to be careful how we manage the game in the Camp Nou.' If he had rehearsed those words, he had rehearsed them very well.

The Barcelona players weren't so placid. Piqué underlined Real's defensive attitude: 'It wasn't as if they stopped playing once they went down to ten men. They weren't even playing before that. The red card? It's always the same argument, when you play with fire in your blood, always playing on the edge, you end up getting burned.' Xavi went further, and hit harder. He was the only player who didn't try to hide his contempt for Mourinho: 'Real took a chance, they kept everyone back and played dirty as they were instructed to by their coach. We were far superior, and we were far superior on the pitch. Football won tonight.' At the same time and in the same place, the Bernabéu mixed zone, Real's players were arguing the exact opposite, according to Mou's instructions. There was one significant exception: Cristiano Ronaldo. The Portuguese superstar complained about Pepe's red card like everyone else, but when he was asked about Real's tactics he didn't try to hide his doubts: 'I don't like our defensive style, but I have to adapt because that's the coach's choice. Nil-nil wouldn't have been a bad result, it would have allowed us to play on the counter-attack in the Camp Nou.'

The next day, reading these comments, Mourinho was so furious he nearly threw his desk over. As we know there was never a great deal of fondness between him and Cristiano, inevitable when they are two cocks in the same henhouse, and Jorge Mendes – in many ways the master of both their careers – had kept them separate for as long as possible. When it was clear to him that Ronaldo risked vanishing in the vast shadow of Messi and his Barcelona side, Mendes was forced to support Florentino Pérez's move to appoint Mourinho, accompanying it with a number of very diplomatic statements, but no less explicit for that, on his two clients. Now that they were part of the same team they needed to support each other, without thinking about who was top dog, because there would only be one result: they would either win or lose together. By this reasoning, José felt betrayed by Cristiano's consideration that Real Madrid were playing too defensively. It would have been serious at any time, but to hear him express those thoughts at the moment in which he, using a very precise strategy, had shifted the entire responsibility for the defeat onto the referee, convinced him once again of Ronaldo's egotism (though, arguably, Mourinho's absolution of responsibility for the defeat was evidence of his own egotism). In his heart – though Mourinho warned him against it – he wanted to be managed by Guardiola, the coach whose attacking style gave his bitter rival Messi five goalscoring chances a game. José didn't call Cristiano into his office, as his instinct would tell him to. He would (almost) never take an immediate decision based on his gut feeling, instead it would be well thought through and calculated. The next day, Friday 29 April, the day before the home La Liga match against Real Zaragoza, Ronaldo wasn't included in the squad. If it was anyone else everyone would have thought it was a natural opportunity for a rest: the league was over by this point, it would be better to hold players back for the second leg of the Champions League the following Wednesday. But Cristiano, like Messi, was never rested, because the Pichichi trophy – for La Liga's top goalscorer – was an objective that was as important to him as the league itself: it celebrates individuality within a team sport, and modern marketing techniques dictated that various t-shirts celebrating the winner would be printed. At that point Messi led the goalscoring charts with 31, two more than Ronaldo: to miss a game, especially one against a mid-table opponent like Zaragoza, meant passing up an opportunity to increase his tally, perhaps considerably. When he found out the news, clearly a punishment for his comments, Cristiano began kicking his locker in the dressing room until it was completely destroyed, in front of the astonished faces of his team-mates.

ELEVEN

LET'S TAKE A STEP BACK, TO THE THURSDAY
after the Champions League first leg. Barcelona had decided not
to let the '*por qué*' of Mourinho slide: they filed a complaint
about the Portuguese coach to UEFA, saying that his allegations
had tarnished the Champions League they won in 2009. In the
Catalan club's statement, they also added that Real had refused
to water the pitch an hour before kick-off, as had been agreed
with the UEFA official, and to read the safety instructions over
the stadium tannoy in Catalan. The final complaint was clearly
political, because Barcelona's supporters understand Castilian
perfectly well and therefore reading the information out in
Catalan was simply on a point of principle. The complaint about
Mourinho, however, was a 'serious' matter, which the club tried

to balance out by excluding Real from the dispute: the rapport between the clubs was defined as satisfactory, 'but there are certain things we cannot allow to pass, because we are proud of our team and our coach'. Naturally though it was impossible to separate Mourinho from Real Madrid, and four hours after Barcelona's statement came Real's reply. It was a formal complaint against the conduct of Barcelona's players, accusing them of continually simulating in order to mislead the referee, which they succeeded in by getting Pepe sent off, and which they would appeal against. Real explicitly took a similar position to Barcelona, 'who want to see our coach punished for exercising freedom of expression.'

On Monday 2 May, the day before the second leg of the semi-final, UEFA announced that they had rejected both complaints. Real's was rejected as they had no grounds for appeal: UEFA could not find evidence of a simulation strategy from Barça, and upheld Stark's decision to send off Pepe by suspending him for one match. Barcelona's was rejected because UEFA's own disciplinary procedure was already underway against Mourinho, as his sequence of 'por qué' had hit a nerve with them: Mourinho was of course suspended for the second leg, and a few days later he would be given a five-match ban (the final game would be a conditional ban) and a €50,000 fine. After the second leg, they rejected another complaint filed against Busquets for racist remarks towards Marcelo. Curiously, Real have always denied filing that complaint, claiming that it was initiated by UEFA itself.

The legal battle was a vulgar but inevitable side-effect of Mourinho's strategy of total war. Ultimately, he had announced his objectives right from the day Europe's top coaches convened in Nyon the previous September. 'Barcelona draw you into the trap of thinking that they are all likeable, nice, friendly people from a perfect world. They try to make you think that they don't buy players, that they develop them all in their youth team...and some people truly believe that.' That day in Nyon, Mourinho, fresh from his Champions League victory with Inter and recently appointed the coach of Real, had behaved with subtle friendliness towards Guardiola, shaking his hand and giving him friendly pats on the back – which everyone saw – while they chatted with Michel Platini. Pep had reacted with a certain degree of discomfort, reluctant to make physical contact, so much so that the Madrid press surreptitiously accused him of being bad-mannered ('why did he hesitate before shaking hands?') while the Barcelona media – on the front pages – warned him not to trust the Portuguese's smile. A harbinger of what was to come in the spring.

On Saturday 30 April, Real Madrid, eight points behind Barça with five league games to go, kicked off first and lost. Mourinho chose his second string, including the attacking trio of Kaká, Higuaín and Benzema, who were beaten 3-2 at home by Real Zaragoza, who took a big step towards avoiding relegation with these unexpected three points. The match finished just before 8pm, when eyes turned towards Barcelona as they took to the pitch at the Anoeta, Real Sociedad's home in San Sebastián and a ground that they had always struggled on – in fact they would lose this game as well, boosted by the knowledge of what had happened at the Bernabéu. Barça scored first through Thiago but then went behind to goals from Ifran and Xabi Prieto. Guardiola had only picked Messi, Xavi and Piqué from his first team, while on the opposite team, even though he didn't score, the burgeoning talent of Antoine Griezmann stood out. We would hear much more from him in later years. With one game fewer remaining, the results edged Barça closer to the Liga title, and everything was now set for the final game in the series of four Clásicos: the second leg of the Champions League semi-final, scheduled for Tuesday 3 May. But Real first had to deal with the highly controversial confrontation between Mou and Ronaldo, and a highly unusual request from the coach to his team.

This back story doesn't come from me, but from the afore-mentioned Diego Torres, the excellent *El País* journalist, and it's worth reiterating his opposition to Mourinho and his methods. In his book *Preparense Para Perder* (*Prepare to Lose*), Diego claims that José, in his team meeting on 1 May, essentially asked his team to play for a 0-0 draw, without trying to mount an impossible comeback. The reasoning for this was to be able to keep accusing Stark of deciding the semi-final by sending off Pepe; if Real had lost badly at the Camp Nou, he would have no more excuses. Moreover, Torres added that later on in the meeting, Mourinho savagely attacked Ronaldo, saying that if the squad had to play deeper it was because he wasn't helping his team-mates by doing his defensive duties, and that only his friendship with Mendes ensured that he wouldn't take even more drastic measures in what was a dead rubber. According to the *El País* journalist, a large part of the team – without openly saying so – reacted badly to the coach's instructions, because Real Madrid are a team who always play to win, not get involved in machinations. Ronaldo, meanwhile, reacted angrily, shouting all manner of things at the coach, who meanwhile was continuing to coldly enumerate on his flaws, his egotism most of all. One curious thing about that summit was that it was the first (and, for a while, the last) that was attended by Zinedine Zidane who, as we've seen, was being imposed as a liaison by Mourinho between the president and the team in place of Jorge Valdano, who was heading towards the exit by now. Torres recounts that at the end of the meeting, Mou suggested to Zizou that he speak freely on the subject in front of the squad, confident of his open support; the Frenchman, however, said the exact opposite – 'you're fantastic players, so you should try to beat Barcelona because Real try to win every game' – earning himself a cold stare from the coach. Zidane, who gave his unconditional support to Florentino Pérez right from his first day in Madrid, reported the content of the meeting to the president, and even he is said not to have liked the order not to try to win, but if so then he didn't show it, because he didn't give any counter-orders to the players. In fact, on the eve of the match, Mourinho and Florentino had a long, very visible discussion in the lobby of the Rey Juan Carlos I Hotel in Barcelona, 500 metres from the Camp Nou, where the team were preparing for the game, at the end of which the coach reiterated his plan to his players: we'll protect this score, keep things tight, then complain afterwards.

The hotel in which Real were waiting for their final ordeal was a characterless skyscraper that UEFA had also chosen as their Barcelona headquarters: the organisation's representatives slept in the same hotel as the away side, as well as the event's sponsors and TV executives. During Real's 36-hour stay, Mourinho didn't leave the hotel: not only did he not attend the final training session, at the end of which Karanka reiterated the accusations against the referee, Barcelona and UEFA for him ('everyone talks about fair play and then they pretend that everything's alright'), he didn't go to the game either. He stayed to watch it in his room on the top floor, peering out of his window at the lights of the Camp Nou every so often and smiling to himself at the vast number of the day's stories dedicated by the media to the way in which the Blaugrana had arranged a seat in the stands for him, which was quite reasonably protected from any potential trouble that might be caused by angry Culés. He didn't need it. Today all he needed was room service. He had made sure there was a small reminder of his absence though: Karanka and Rui Faria wouldn't sit next to each other on the bench, but instead would leave an empty seat between them.

To make the contrast between Real's anger and Barça's innocence even clearer, Guardiola used his press conference to announce Eric Abidal's return to the bench 46 days after his operation to have a tumour removed from his liver. It was fantastic news, but the polarisation of the moods of the two camps caused many Mourinhisti to consider it another pretence, yet another made up element of a story aimed at magnifying Barça's apparent humanity. Guardiola, smiling and focused, reiterated these values by commenting on UEFA's absolution of his players accused of diving and racist remarks: 'I never doubted anyone. The guys who develop at this club don't just receive a sporting education, but an ethical one too. And UEFA have confirmed that.'

No comment on his opponents? Well, just one. Accompanied by an obvious sign of relief.

'I'm happy that this sequence of games is nearly over, I couldn't face Real Madrid again.' If he was being completely honest, he should have said Mourinho's name instead of the club.

Rain fell incessantly on Barcelona throughout that Tuesday, almost as if it was needed to cleanse the stains that had sullied all of the other games. From a technical perspective, the fourth Clásico was the best, because Real's team – almost necessarily due to Pepe and Ramos' suspensions – finally fully utilised the squad's exceptional quality. The usual 4-3-3 became a 4-2-3-1, which allowed them to play a recognised centre forward, Gonzalo Higuaín, with a trio of the highest quality behind him: Ronaldo, Kaká and Di María. It wasn't a team that was designed to defend, and the general consensus was that, in the end, Florentino had intervened. Naturally there was a questionable refereeing decision in this game as well: it happened just after half time, when the score was still 0-0. Cristiano led a rapid counter attack and he and Piqué went shoulder to shoulder just as he gave the ball to Higuaín to shoot. It wasn't a foul, but as he fell Ronaldo tripped Mascherano, who was trying to chase after Higuaín: the effect it had was undeniable, but it was equally clear that the defender wasn't going to catch up with the striker. Ultimately, it was the classic situation where Blaugrana supporters claimed it was the correct decision and Madridistas claimed they had been robbed. What do you think the chances were that Karanka would even touch on a subject other than this decision by De Bleeckere in his post-match press conference...The 965 accredited journalists did, and were more or less unanimous in pointing out that this was a Real Madrid team that was finally in keeping with the club's tradition, adding that Mourinho would have done better by having more confidence in his own players and dropping the mind games about referees.

It ended in a draw, after Pedro's opener was cancelled out by

Marcelo, and the draw was an entirely fair result, which Barcelona celebrated by bringing on Abidal, who prayed next to the
bench before coming on, for a highly significant two minutes at
the end. Cancer had suddenly had a huge effect on the Catalans,
and would tragically continue to do so over the course of the
next three seasons, since the French full-back suffered a relapse
– his life was saved by a liver transplant – and most of all when
Tito Vilanova, who took over Pep Guardiola's squad and won a
league title, passed away in spring 2014 following a battle with a
rare form of throat cancer.

EPILOGUE

IT'S FIVE YEARS BEFORE THE 18 DAYS.

It's the evening of 6 March, 2006, and the full moon is shining on Barcelona's Port Olímpic. The temperature is already at least fifteen degrees – spring always comes quickly in Catalonia – and, after dinner time, the sliding doors of the Hotel Arts opened to let out a small group of men wearing Chelsea tracksuits. It was the day before the second leg of their Champions League Round of 16 tie: Barcelona had won a highly controversial first leg 2-1 at Stamford Bridge, because when it was 0-0 the English team's Basque left back, Asier Del Horno, was sent off for a foul on Leo Messi, and Mourinho had accused the Argentine of diving. 'It was top quality play-acting. Besides, I've lived with you, in Barcelona, and I know all about your taste for the theatre.' For a neutral, his sarcasm was entertaining, but it came across as arrogant to the Catalan journalists, who heard him repeat it in the press room during his pre-match press conference. But his comments hadn't yet spread far across the radio, and so even though the Culés had begun disliking him the previous year, when Chelsea had knocked out Barça, José could still leave his hotel to go for a drink with his staff before going to bed. Incidentally, Del Horno's challenge on Messi was violent but Leo, anticipating the impact, was able to avoid serious injury. So although the way in which he rolled around inconsolably on the ground was over the top, it turned out to be exactly the same as the Pepe-Dani Alves incident; the red card was warranted, but the way the players feigned injury also deserved to be criticised.

At the time of his trip to the port, Mourinho's assistants weren't recognisable but, looking back at it with the benefit of hindsight, it's possible to identify two of the three people accompanying him that night as André Villas Boas and Rui Faria. Fate sent the four of them strolling down to the harbour, lazily gazing at the boats that were moored up, at the same time as I was coming out of a restaurant; even though we didn't know each other – not at the time – I have to confess that, by holding a few metres back, I eavesdropped on their conversation for a few minutes. There were no big secrets, nor did they say anything controversial about anyone: it was mostly Mourinho who spoke, recounting the four years he had spent in Catalonia between 1996 and 2000, pointing out a spot a long way down the coast at Sitges where he had once had a house, the Olympic village – located just behind the port – and commenting how nice it was when it was new (though it is now in less good shape), indicating the pier where one high-ranking Blaugrana director kept his yacht, and telling various unimportant stories about the good memories he had of his time in a city and an atmosphere that he had hugely enjoyed. He really was gushing with absolute love and respect for the city and the football club of Barcelona. Every time across the years that José has tried to find the most radical opposing position to Barcelona, I think back to those words I overheard in 2006, of how enamoured he was, and of a dream he once had but which has become increasingly distant over time (never say never, but after so much controversy it would be incredibly difficult...), which has left him with exceedingly bitter thoughts.

Does Mourinho hate Barcelona because he was never able to go back there to become first team coach? Does Mourinho hate Guardiola because he was appointed coach instead of him just at the point when the club began its extraordinary period of success? Many people believe these arguments, which are based on contact that was made back in 2008 and was reported at the time, and which were recently confirmed by Ferran Soriano, now a director at Manchester City but who was at Barça at the time, in his book. In the spring of that year, before talks with Inter began, two Barcelona directors went to talk to José at his house in Portugal about taking on the role of coach.

Many candidates were initially considered to be Rijkaard's replacement, but the list was rapidly shortened to just two names: José Mourinho and Pep Guardiola. A world famous coach, who had already won league titles and European trophies, and an apprentice, who had undoubted charisma but who also only had one season of experience in the third division with Barcelona B. When the Portuguese, with the strong backing of a sizeable part of the club's management and, subtly, from *Mundo Deportivo*, seemed to be on the verge of being appointed, Johan Cruyff, whose influence on that management team was undoubtedly very important, appealed to president Laporta to take an alternative course of action. Cruyff argued that Mourinho played a style of football that was too far removed from the club's tactical orthodoxy, and that when things got tough his priority was to defend himself and his image before thinking about the good of the club. Two days after his intervention, Laporta invited Guardiola to lunch, and when Pep provoked him by telling him that he would never have the courage to appoint him, the president reached into his briefcase and took out the pre-prepared contract.

There's enough evidence to suggest Mourinho is something of a fallen angel from the Catalan paradise, but was this enough to spark the fire within him? In the years that he worked there, initially as Bobby Robson's translator, then his assistant, and then as van Gaal's number two, José lived side by side with the Dutchman, recently in charge of Manchester United, and of course with Guardiola, with Luis Enrique, Barcelona's current coach, and with other noteworthy coaches like Laurent Blanc, Phillip Cocu, Frank de Boer, Ronald Koeman, Julen Lopetegui. These men don't all coach their teams to play the same way, but there is clearly a shared background between them all, demonstrating that in the mid-90s, Barcelona was definitely the most prestigious football university in the world. It was the Harvard of football. When Guardiola issued his sibylline warning – 'he knows me, I know him' – to imply that there were all sorts of secrets waiting to be told, it was in fact a reference to a form of Catalan obedience, or perhaps respect is a more appropriate term. But Mourinho didn't know what to do with that respect, just as he didn't know what to do with the dignity of Real Madrid: he is a deviant Jedi knight, he is the Darth Vader seduced by the dark side of the Force. José only wants to win, and only learned the practical advice from his lessons in Catalonia. Van Gaal recognised this after getting to know him and realising that his advice turned out to be much more effective than that of his other assistants. In an admiring tone, much less arrogant than usual, the Dutchman confessed that the Portuguese was different – he was a man who would follow his pragmatism regardless of the consequences.

While knowing little about psychoanalysis, I imagine that causing controversy about Del Horno's red card or having seen Rijkaard talking in a low voice with Anders Frisk at half-time were ways for him to 'kill his father' in football terms. After achieving his aim, Mourinho was absolutely ready to take on the role of leading the team of his dreams and the club of his youth. The fact that they rejected him, and even accused him of not being one of them, made him fly into a rage. Since then José has continued his career as a coach in search of vindication, and there's no doubt that the highlight of Inter's great performance at the Camp Nou, perhaps the key to victory in his eyes, was the incident with the sprinklers, which came on while the Inter players were still celebrating on the pitch after reaching the final. It was a revealing moment, showing that even Barcelona don't have the perfect Corinthian spirit they are often suggested to have. Or, in the words of an old fox like Mircea Lucescu, that they are only sportsmanlike when they win. Mourinho was aiming high, to show the world that despite their nature, Barcelona – the club who had rejected him in obedience to their motto *'mes que un club*' – didn't have a trophy to parade alongside their supposed moral superiority. They're not the good guys, José shouts, splitting hairs over every detail, intolerant of the vulgar idea that generosity implies talent and therefore success: the subtlety of his reference to UNICEF as a possible sponsor of victory by proxy, as if referees would give them decisions after being moved by the thought of poor children, was telling.

It was a strategy of total war that José would continue to maintain.

As Jonathan Wilson noted in his long article 'The Devil and José Mourinho', in his press conference after winning the Premier League title with Chelsea in 2015, instead of celebrating his great achievement, thanking the players and describing his own triumph – the classic topics after winning the league – he decided that it would be better to attack Guardiola, even though he didn't explicitly name him: 'I'm not the smartest guy to choose countries and clubs. I could choose another club in another country where to be champion is easier. Instead I accepted the risk of a more equally balanced tournament, and I'm so, so happy to have won it. I was champion at every club I coached: Inter, Real Madrid, and twice at Chelsea. I couldn't pick one, they're all important, to win the title with Real with 100 points against the best Barcelona team ever was a big achievement. Maybe in the future I have to be smarter and choose another club in another country where everybody is champion. Maybe I will go to a country where a kit man can be coach and win the title. Sooner or later I'll decide to do it, but it won't be now because I still enjoy these difficulties.' The reference to Guardiola and the 'ease' with which he excelled in the Bundesliga in the previous three seasons was blatant.

The ambition that Mourinho showed in spring 2016 to become the new Manchester United manager could equally be seen as the search for a new battleground for a direct confrontation with Pep – even if it would be of limited historic significance, unlike the four Clásicos – a battleground that he had been absent from ever since the European Super Cup in summer 2013. That evening in Prague it was Guardiola who won, securing his first trophy with Bayern, in Mourinho's first big game after he had taken charge of Chelsea for the second time. It was a spectacular, entertaining game, an unusually open game for that time in the season, which Pep won on penalties after Javi Martínez had equalised in the 121st minute. At that point Mou turned towards the Bavarian bench and made the universal gesture of fortune. He could afford to because he was right, and because the pleasant August climate was hardly conducive to high drama. Even so, Chelsea's Brazilian Ramires was still sent off for a second yellow card (for a foul on Mario Götze) towards the end of normal time, which allowed José to make the obvious joke in the dressing room about the fact that it's impossible to play against a Guardiola team without finishing the game with a numerical disadvantage.

While the game in Prague was the 16th head-to-head match between them, the frenzy – partly stoked by the media – with which Mou pursued the United job was a sign of his desire to raise the stakes once again. At the time Manchester United weren't at their peak, and making Manchester the arena for the new duel – Guardiola had long since announced he would be joining Manchester City – would be equivalent to building a cage around him. José has looked for personal contact right from the start, exactly like Feraud with d'Hubert, and the idea that they could cross paths in a restaurant, in a shop, even taking their dogs for a walk, exhilarated him because he knew that it would make Pep stressed and annoyed.

'When a coach of the calibre of Mourinho arrives, it makes us all better,' Guardiola had said, in a desperate search for normality, when he was asked to comment on José's appointment at Real Madrid. However, at the end of the series of four Clásicos in eighteen days – a series he won convincingly, because Barcelona saw off Manchester United relatively easily in the final at Wembley, so while he held La Liga and Champions League titles at the end of the season, Mourinho just had the Copa del Rey in his hands – his words were tired and depressed. 'These aren't games that I will remember fondly, regardless of the results, because they were accompanied by too many incidents that are incomprehensible to me. I think, ultimately, Mourinho has won the war.' And within this last phrase is all the bitterness for a confrontation that he would have liked to contest at a higher level, but which he was instead forced to contest at José's level by entering into a mudslinging contest: the 'fucking boss' press conference, for example, was seen by Pep as a descent into the underworld. It was necessary at the time, but it should never be repeated – in fact, which should be forgotten, if possible – because it was too far removed from his self-imposed stylistic image.

It's interesting, and far from misleading, to look for comparisons between the most stimulating duellists in the world of football – the intellectual level of their rivalry is unmatched in football, and is very close to the likes of Karpov-Kasparov – and the *Star Wars* saga, because if José Mourinho is a perfect Darth

Vader, or rather a perfect Anakin Skywalker who transforms into Darth Vader, Pep Guardiola is very reminiscent of Obi-Wan Kenobi. As the saga develops, the erstwhile friends end up fighting to the death, and while Obi-Wan initially has the upper hand over his disciple (*Revenge of the Sith*), in the end Darth Vader prevails (*A New Hope*). In the same way, although Guardiola won the 18-day war, it was his swansong in Catalonia. Exhausted by the harshness of the conflict and poisoned by his rival, he collapsed the next season as his team finished nine points behind Real in La Liga. The critical moment came in the spring when he was beaten at home, in convincing style, in a head-to-head clash that could have revitalised the title challenge. Both teams went out eventfully in the Champions League semi-finals, Real on penalties to Bayern and Barça to Chelsea when it had seemed all but over: clearly, all of their energy had been used up in the league.

And at that point Guardiola quit football for a year's sabbatical, a decision that left the entire football world dumbfounded. But it was a wise choice, because he really had nothing left to give at that point, and he needed peace and time to reconsider his relationship with football. Just think about how the battle with Mourinho had shaken him to the core. Meanwhile, deprived of the rival who in a way had consecrated his own career, José became a different man and a different coach: distracted, distant, emptied of the adrenaline that had made him a war machine. He was forced to endure Tito Vilanova's perfect season – his short-lived happy season in charge of Barça – in La Liga, while he was made to pay for the awful evening in Dortmund in the Champions League, and he was even beaten in the in the Copa del Rey final by the nascent Atletico Madrid of Diego Simeone. He would call it 'the worst season of my career', and terminated his contract with Real by mutual consent. A season – we should add – in which he suffered terribly from the absence of his favourite enemy. Because in the end, that is the real treasure, the real richness that transforms lives and careers: an opponent – whether it's an enemy, rival or adversary ultimately doesn't matter – who forces you to give your best, on pain of defeat.

STATISTICS

LA LIGA
REAL MADRID V BARCELONA 16 APRIL 2011
VENUE: BERNABÉU. ATTENDANCE: 80,000. SCORE: 1-1

Real Madrid

Iker Casillas, Pepe, Marcelo, Ricardo Carvalho, Sergio Ramos, Raúl Albiol, Xabi Alonso (off 67'), Ángel di María (off 67'), Sami Khedira, Karim Benzema (off 57'), Cristiano Ronaldo.
Substitutes: Antonio Adán, Ezequiel Garay, Álvaro Arbeloa (on 67'), Kaká, Mesut Özil (on 57'), Emmanuel Adebayor (on 67'), Gonzalo Higuían.
Goal: Cristiano Ronaldo 82' (penalty).
Yellow cards: 2 – Marcelo 31', Arbeloa 76'; *Red cards:* 1 – Albiol 52'

Barcelona

Victor Valdés, Dani Alves, Gerard Piqué, Adriano (off 80'), Carles Puyol (off 58'), Pedro (off 67'), Andrés Iniesta, Xavi Hernández, Sergio Busquets, Lionel Messi, David Villa.
Substitutes: Pinto, Maxwell (on 80'), Gabriel Milito, Andreu Fontàs, Thiago Alcântara Ibrahim Afellay (on 67'), Seydou Kéita (on 58').
Goal: Lionel Messi 53' (penalty).
Yellow cards: 5 – Adriano, Piqué 27', Alves 79', Victor Valdés 81', Xavi 90'+; *Red cards:* 0

COPA DEL REY FINAL
BARCELONA V REAL MADRID 20 APRIL 2011
VENUE: MESTALLA. ATTENDANCE: 55,000. SCORE: 0-1

Barcelona

Pinto, Adriano (off 120'+), Gerard Piqué, Dani Alves, Sergio Busquets (off 108'), Andrés Iniesta, Xavi Hernandez, Javier Mascherano, Pedro, David Villa (off 106'), Lionel Messi.
Substitutes: Victor Valdés, Maxwell (on 120'+), Carles Puyol, Gabriel Milito, Ibrahim Afellay (on 106'), Thiago Alcântara, Seydou Kéita (on 108').
Yellow cards: 3 – Pedro 30', Messi 64', Adriano 118'; *Red cards:* 0

Real Madrid

Iker Casillas, Ricardo Carvalho (off 119'), Pepe, Marcelo, Sergio Ramos, Álvaro Arbeloa, Sami Khedira (off 104'), Ángel di María, Xabi Alonso, Mesut Özil (off 70'), Cristiano Ronaldo.
Substitutes: Jerzy Dudek, Ezequiel Garay (on 119'), Esteban Granero (on 104'), Kaká, Emmanuel Adebayor (on 70'), Gonzalo Higuaín, Karim Benzema.
Goal: Cristiano Ronaldo 103'.
Yellow cards: 5 – Pepe 26', Alonso 60', Adebayor 74', di María 86' 120'+;
Red cards: 1 – di María 120'+

CHAMPIONS LEAGUE SEMI-FINAL (1ST LEG)
REAL MADRID V BARCELONA, 27 APRIL 2011
VENUE: BERNABÉU. ATTENDANCE: 71,567. SCORE: 0-2

Real Madrid

Iker Casillas, Marcelo, Raúl Albiol, Pepe, Álvaro Arbeloa, Sergio Ramos, Ángel di María, Lassana Diarra, Mesut Özil (off 46'), Xabi Alonso, Cristiano Ronaldo.
Substitutes: Antonio Adán, Ezequiel Garay, Kaká, Esteban Granero, Emmanuel Adebayor (on 46'), Gonzalo Higuaín, Karim Benzema.
Yellow cards: 33 –Arbeloa 40', Ramos 53', Adebayor 83'; *Red cards:* 1 – Pepe 61'

Barcelona

Victor Valdés, Gerard Piqué, Dani Alves, Carles Puyol, Javier Mascherano, Xavi, Seydou Kéita, Sergio Busquets, Pedro (off 71'), David Villa (off 90'), Lionel Messi.
Substitutes: Pinto, Gabriel Milito, Adnreu Fontàs, Sergi Roberto (on 90'), Ibrahim Afellay (on 71'), Thiago Alcântara, Jeffren Suárez.
Goals: Lionel Messi, 76' 87'.
Yellow cards: 2 – Alves 44', Mascherano 57'; *Red cards:* 1 – Pinto 45'+

CHAMPIONS LEAGUE SEMI-FINAL (2ND LEG)
BARCELONA V REAL MADRID. 3 MAY 2011
VENUE: CAMP NOU. ATTENDANCE: 95,701. SCORE: 1-1

Barcelona

Victor Valdés, Dani Alves, Carles Puyol (off 90'+), Gerard Piqué, Javier Mascherano, Sergio Busquets, Pedro (off 90'+), Andrés Iniesta, Xavi Hernández, David Villa (off 74'), Lionel Messi.
Substitutes: Oier Olazábal, Éric Abidal (on 90'+), Andreu Fontàs, Ibrahim Afellay (on 90'+), Thiago Alcântara, Seydou Kéita (on 74'), Jeffren Suárez.
Goal: Pedro 54'.
Yellow cards: 1 – Pedro 82'; *Red cards:* 0

Real Madrid

Iker Casillas, Ricardo Carvalho, Álvaro Arbeloa, Marcelo, Raúl Albiol, Lassana Diarra, Xabi Alonso, Ángel di María, Kaká (off 60'), Gonzalo Higuaín (off 55'), Cristiano Ronaldo.
Substitutes: Jerzy Dudek, Ezequiel Garay, Nacho, Esteban Granero, Mesut Özil (on 60'), Emmanuel Adebayor (on 55'), Karim Benzema.
Goal: Marcelo 64'.
Yellow cards: 5 – Carvalho 13', Diarra 58', Alonso 69', Marcelo 76', Adebayor 85'; *Red cards:* 0